Thomas Francis Crosse

On the Giving of the Hebrew Law

Thomas Francis Crosse

On the Giving of the Hebrew Law

ISBN/EAN: 9783337316686

Printed in Europe, USA, Canada, Australia, Japan

Cover: Foto ©Suzi / pixelio.de

More available books at **www.hansebooks.com**

THE

HEBREW LAW.

BY THE SAME AUTHOR.

---◆---

LECTURES ON EARLY SCRIPTURE.

Price 5s.

London: LONGMANS & CO.

ON

THE GIVING

OF THE

HEBREW LAW.

BY

T. F. CROSSE, D.C.L.

MEMBER OF THE HON. SOCIETY OF THE INNER TEMPLE.

INCUMBENT OF HOLY TRINITY AND RURAL DEAN OF HASTINGS.

LONDON:

LONGMANS, GREEN, AND CO.

1875.

LONDON : PRINTED BY
SPOTTISWOODE AND CO., NEW-STREET SQUARE
AND PARLIAMENT STREET

PREFACE.

———◇◆◇———

THIS BOOK upon the giving of the Hebrew
Law is the continuation of another called
'Lectures on Early Scripture,' and is intended,
like that, to point out the unity of design
which pervades the plan and incidents of the
Bible, and so to suggest and assist towards a
way of looking at the System of the Holy
Scriptures which may, by the Divine Blessing,
be of service to enquirers.

CONTENTS.

viii   Contents.

HEBREW LAW.

CHAPTER I.

THE original beginnings of legal order, and
their relation to religion, have been often
inquired about and in different ways. It might
naturally be supposed that, in such matters,
considerations on the divine Author of religion
and society must count for much, and that
starting with a fixed impression as to His
unity and His character, drawn from what
we can observe within us and around us, we
should use that as a great foundation of reserve
through which both to deduce and test our
conclusions, since it appears evident enough
that if there be a Divinity at all with such
wide-reaching qualities and functions as we
attribute to Him, He must necessarily be at
the head and source of law. So fully does

this seem the case that the effort to investi-
gate moral foundations, apart from God,
appears to common believers as arbitrary and
artificial as would be an attempt to examine
nature apart from light and heat, or an attempt
to explain the British constitution without reference to the office of king.

Such an errant course, however, as regards
law has not unfrequently been engaged in.
Indeed so closely inherent is the instinct of
liberty in the human mind that the tendency,
even among some inquirers of justice and
integrity, has rather been to aim at shutting
out prepossessions, however reverent, and letting the mind collect, weigh, and decide for
itself without any bias of authority. In following out this tendency, however, two defective methods have come into use. The first
of these is an avoidance of metaphysical and
moral grounds of argument as if they were
something untrustworthy, although it is evident that law, which is so mixed up with these
ingredients, cannot be fully considered without
reference to them. The second is that when
pursuing the method they have preferred—

that of examining phenomena—these inquirers
have only partially applied their own tests;
that is, they have neglected Hebrew antiquities,
and drawn their inferences chiefly from Hindoo,
classic, and northern remains. Now, it seems
hardly just, when one has started upon a
purely independent scientific investigation, and
has professed to be prepared to follow wherever scientific research may lead, ar d when one
has selected a certain set of witnesses as those
whom science requires to have examined, that
then he should refuse to call the chief of these
—that while the East, the North, and the West
are successively ransacked, and all sorts of
minute fragments collected together from them
and dovetailed into an expressive shape, the
most venerable centre should alone remain
unvisited, and that Hebrew antiquities, which
so many and various races have been impressed
by, should alone be shut out from speaking.
It is evident that no generalisation of such sort
can be held complete, but that every true
representation of the testimony of antiquity
must give as full effect to the inferences resulting from Hebrew remains as to others; for,

even independent of their peculiar pretensions, these remains are certainly of great antiquarian value.

But passing this, it may be questioned how far the investigations of a supposed scientific character, which now find such favour with some, are, after all, of value in religion. The supply of facts is at present small. The applications are unfamiliar and partial. The position is constrained in consequence of the forced rejection from examination of those very documents of revelation the world has long looked to as throwing the most important light on the matter. The temptation is greater than usual to anticipate conclusions. There is a disadvantage in judging results from not being able to have recourse to those tests which in physical science so quickly reduce back vagrant speculations within safe bounds. When we consider all these difficulties with which such a method is hampered, we may well feel that those who profess not merely to shed rays of new light from such sources upon questions of the most vital and practical interest to mankind, but to introduce altogether strange views about them, should be very careful—more careful, indeed, than some of them have been—how they un-settle opinion and sow doubt, when their own theories must be open to such grave question. It is quite open to inquiry, we repeat, whether there is not a considerable amount of self-deception as to the value of such researches, and whether it may not be very doubtful if those who come after us will endorse, with the same readiness as some of ourselves, the speculations which rest on such frail foundations. Sir William Jones long ago complained of the attempt of the students of words to prove everything by the structure of language, and the same may be objected to the sociologist, legist, and even to the theologian, when their efforts are but one-sided and exclusive.

There may be additional reason, too, for our hesitating to give rapid and implicit ad-herence to philosophers of the above class in the fact that they are met and encountered by yet another body of philosophers, equally high in pretensions, and equally unprejudiced as regards orthodox beliefs, who declare loudly that all such researches are illusory ; that the

method of investigation is vain; the conclusions derived from it utterly incorrect; and
that even if it were possible thus to draw up
and piece together again the old fragments, so
as to reproduce something like the portraiture
of the most ancient life really taken from those
who lived it themselves, yet that those ages
were so completely unable to conceive things
in their actual relations, and so totally without
the historical sense, that their impressions of
themselves would be worth next to nothing at
all. And this criticism has, perhaps, rather
the more force from its being used by those
who are usually in favour of experimental
inductions, and who do not so much object
here to the method itself as to its application
in the case of archaic religion and law.

While whole schools of thought are thus at
variance, it may be permitted to ordinary
people to go on reasoning as they have
always hitherto reasoned, making use, to some
extent, indifferently of the above ways of
thinking, and also of other ways besides, and
yet bringing them all into contact with those
primary convictions about God and man, and

the world, which, if they be in any degree
prejudices, as some would persuade us, are yet,
in a very great degree and in the best sense,
philosophical truths. For surely the general
convictions of all ages, the widest observations
of the natural world, the impressions and
expressions of universal feeling, are not to be
treated as on the outside of philosophy. They
are rather the very materials philosophers are
in search of—the very voice they are desiring
to listen to; and the observation of them is
the very process they are actually applying in
another and less valuable series of materials.
The direct historical statements, the current
opinions, the general social attitude of remote
ages, should be taken together as one wide
declaration of belief. So interpreted, they are
relics of a direct, tangible, and most valuable
character. Inferences from mental states and
movements, when thus of a comprehensive
character, are distinct and realistic results.
They are far superior in evidential weight to
mere chippings and fragments, the real place
of which in the scale is doubtful, but which
are made sometimes the unstable fulcrum of

movement not so much scientific as merely unfriendly to established beliefs.

On the other hand, when we see pressed together the many little morsels which mere secular observation can supply, and when we see the effort made to shut out additions from all other quarters, we know that from such sources alone no complete system can be obtained, no theory can be built up which will at all account for, or correspond to, what has been, is, and should be in the world within us and in the world around us. Minute researches of this sort are often very ingenious in themselves, and have the sort of value in pointing and hinting which the little signs known to woodcraft have in a forest labyrinth, but they are not, and never can be, the map on which the whole area of the vast subject is to be found set out, and by which it can be comprehended, subdued, and utilised. Such researches, therefore, are but ancillary and of secondary value, nor is there any real reason to suppose they do or will yield the results by some persons attributed to them. Materials for induction in theology, whether in its general or dispensational aspects, must be collected from a wider field, and must range not only over matter, but over mind as well. To take a bit of flint, and yet reject an institution ; to analyse a word, and, at the same time, to ignore a manuscript; to construct a past of our own, while repudiating the past as understood by ages much nearer to it than ourselves— these are processes which will never hold. Novelty for a time may make them the mode, but they will hardly in the end realise either the hopes or fears they have awakened. They may dispel some clouds from religion and collect others, but the loftiest truths or theology which are not subjects of induction, will, like the heights of snow mountains, still be found rising steadfastly above them.

In our attempts, then, to examine the superstructure of law, we shall take account also of its foundations. We shall aim at keeping open before us the final source of legislation, and at using it for a guide to the particular legal system. Through that we shall hope to estimate its value, interpret its meaning, calculate its effects, and trace its relations to some wider

and more universal scheme of government, supposing such to exist.   This we shall do chiefly
in the Hebrew, and incidentally in other
theories of law.

If there is a God with qualities such as we
imagine in Him, the final law must be His
will ; and it is assumed here, as we have said,
that such a Divine Being does exist ; that there
is a God, and that He created and constantly
governs the world and all things therein.
Observations supporting this assumption occur
further on in our pages.   At present it may
be enough to suggest that, in taking thus much
for granted, we assume nothing unreasonable,
for that reason possessed by men which has
everywhere formed them into societies, and
arranged and carried on the government of
these by reasonable laws which it has invented
or adapted, has yet nowhere been satisfied to
consider such laws as merely of its own
authority, but has always tried to have it
believed that they rest on some higher sanction, descending to us from the divine sphere.
Since, then, the wisest and most experienced
among men have not been content with their

own power, but have always insisted on defer-
ring to some higher authority on which they
have based their own, we may well take their
admission, and suppose, with them, that there
really is this divine legislative source which
they have felt the need of and believed in.
No doubt, had it been merely a few clever
empirics who had acted in this way, they
might have been suspected of ingeniously
abusing popular prejudice. That, however, is
no longer a conspiracy, but a genuine movement, which is found everywhere and always,
and among those who are without mutual
knowledge or communication.

And, indeed, were this the moment to pass
from experience to theory on the point, we
might ask, what is the meaning of right and
wrong—those pillars of all law—if there be no
supreme divine authority from which to draw
it. Are we to suppose right and wrong as
resting merely upon what is convenient or the
reverse, and therefore not immutable but vary-
ing. Or are we to suppose it is not general
convenience, but the universal conscience of
men (a more truly descriptive expression than

that of "popular prejudice" just used), which
has everywhere accepted some wide principles
of right and wrong? If so, how can we account
for such wide agreement, or for such faculty
for uniform moral result, unless we suppose
some power behind from which man derives
his impulse—a power which, however named
by us, will really be God?

But this question of the existence of the
Divinity need not be made a point at this
moment. A certain number of persons have
been found opposed to it, just as there are
some who have seriously questioned the real
existence of the outer world around them, or
even of themselves; but the immense majority
of men have instinctively allowed it, and it is
to persons of the usual mould that religious
considerations appeal. In all reasoning something must be taken for granted, and nothing
is here more fit to be than this. So completely,
indeed, are most men convinced of the existence
of God, and such elevated and abstract notions
of His qualities have they formed, that it is
even found one of their difficulties in coming
to Revelation that the Scriptural accounts of

God there given do not seem to them sufficiently exalted and superior to human affairs.
Not only, too, do they allow an outer nature-
world, but they fancy it so inflexibly fixed that
their difficulty is to see how such things as
miracles could come into the midst of its
seemingly steadfast order.

Were proof of God's existence required, we
believe an immense and overwhelming body of
it has been provided for us, drawn from the
most varied sources, and all tending to make
an irresistible impression on just and unprejudiced minds. On this evidence it will not be
necessary to enter now : it will be permissible
here to accept as established fact that the
Almighty Being exists; that He made and
sustains His whole creation; that "of Him
and through Him and to Him are all things"
(Rom. xi. 35) ; and that in Him "we live and
move and have our being" (Act xvii. 28).

And when we go on to meditate about the
dealings and character of God thus imagined,
we begin to perceive that we have, through the
very force of terms, to regard His action as
extended and comprehensive in the widest

possible degree, so that every existing thing
has to be conceived as absolutely within His
immediate domain ; that we cannot allow anything whatever to be independent of His rule
and management ; that He holds, as it were,
the whole world in the hollow of His hand,
and that therefore the final root and source of
all law, of which source we were in search,
must of necessity be His will, and that if any
other will is to be supposed as coming in to
modify it in any degree, however slight, that
can only occur by His special arrangement or
allowance.   Thus, then, we have one World-
Governor, and His will the one final law.

But is it not the case when we come to draw
our inferences about God's dealings with nature
that His attributes, as above conceived, seem
to forbid us to suppose of Him that He first
legislated and then left His domain ?   Do we
not seem to find that we are not to look on
Him as an absent, but as a present God ; that
He did not make the world, launch it on its
course, and then leave it, as one winds up a
watch and goes away, but that He is always
with it every moment, guiding it and super-

vising it with incessant indefatigable care, so
that the Psalmist (Ps. civ.) was completely
laying out the truth when, after describing
God's provision for His creatures, he did not
write of it as a mere sumptuary system started
and then trusted to work by itself alone, but,
on the contrary, described all this as being
always doing by incessant applications of pro-
vident power, saying (vv. 26-30), "all these"
— "innumerable things" — "wait all upon
Thee that Thou mayest give them their meat in
due season; that Thou givest them, they gather;
Thou openest Thy hand, they are filled with
good; Thou hidest Thy face, they are troubled;
Thou takest away their breath, they die and
return to their dust; Thou sendest forth Thy
spirit, they are created; and Thou renewest
the face of the earth."

Now, if God's rule be thus an incessant presence and personal action, and if He is never
"sleeping," or "absent on a journey," or
occupied with some matters to the partial
exclusion of the rest, does there not seem to
follow this consequence important for us here
—viz., that all the supposed system commonly

talked of as " natural laws," has not such fully
real existence as commonly supposed, but that
it is, to a great extent, a notion of ours bor-
rowed from our own affairs, and expressed in
our common parlance. In carrying on these
affairs, our limited powers and opportunities
oblige us to begin by settling certain rules
through some concentration of general wisdom,
and these once settled we call law. This law
is thenceforth to us something permanent and
fixed, and towards which our practice has to
work. May it not be that our notions, therefore, run at once, when we come to speak of
world-government, towards something of the
same sort; that we in imagination lend to per-
fection, our own infirmity, and talk of God's
acting on a plan and by a law, because we
ourselves usually do so. Indeed, we are
fatigued by the idea of an universal presence omnipotently willing, and working in
an incessant now. So when we find regu.
larity in the outer world, it better suits our
habits to account for this by supposing a set
of rules made in the past, and continued on
in action by ulterior agencies. For our own

convenience in thinking this artificial method of ours may be well enough; but to invest it, as some have done, with such authority as even to compete with God Himself seems surely something like the conduct of that old Greek who began by carving out the statue of his ideal in stone, and ended by falling in love with it. For, in reality, as we say, the idea we get of God's attributes when it is formed strictly, and is consistently applied by us, seems to require quite a different conclusion—viz., that it is nothing less than His personal and immediate will which is constantly being exercised in each particular of the immense series of cases His system developes; that the exercise of it is uniform, because His mind and purpose remain uniform and unchanged. The resulting work, therefore, presents that fixity of aspect to which we are accustomed as a feature of law, but, as observed, it is because we do not habitually realise His omnipresence, and yet constantly note this regular working, that it appears to us a sufficient account of the matter to speak of it all as law in nature.

This idea, then, of the incessant presence of the Divine Being among all His works may really be the only one which is consistent with His attributes. It is at this point that the sacred poetry of the Scripture (as Ps. xxix.) and the common thinking of philosophy seem to unite, and we have to realise that it is not a law, but a voice, "the voice of the Lord," which "commandeth the waters," "maketh the thunder," "ruleth the sea," "breaketh the cedar trees," "divideth the flames of fire," "shaketh the wilderness," and "maketh the hinds to bring forth"; and that it is in thus believing and thus regarding nature that we "give the Lord the honour due unto His name." Now, if we accept this view, then, our idea of the highest and most final law will be that of a personal will of God continuously exerted by Him, personally present—a method of government not, after all, strange and un-known to human affairs, but which was, in fact, reflected among men in early stages of society by the personal government of patri-archal chiefs, and by the old "paternal"

monarchies, and which was only changed by
degrees for our artificial plans, as it became
necessary to meet the pressing difficulties and
the wants of more complicated civilisation.

Nor is there, perhaps, any essential reason
to disincline us from such a view of nature as
the above, for nature may have some more
close relations to God than is commonly
imagined. It certainly is not something
foreign to Him with which He is dealing
only as a workman deals with materials
independent of him, and supplied from some
distinct source. Nature may, perhaps, rather
be as close to God as the breath to the mouth,
or the garment to the body. It may be as a
glory-cloud surrounding Him, and reflecting
the light of His presence ; a cloud, in the midst
of which He, though unseen, is ever resting
and working—a holy vapour from the central
altar fire, coloured and fed with the brightness
which gives it incessant birth and increase.

Let it, then, be supposed that nature, or the
laws of nature, are not inflexible and necessarily invariable, as sometimes imagined, but
liable to change on any fitting occasion, because

they are so many individual actions of Him
whose conduct is always fitted to the occasion.
Let it further be remembered that the physical
records of the ancient earth supply much evidence of orders of nature very different from
the present ; methods which seem to have long
existed, and then to have been gradually or
suddenly changed and broken in upon.   Let
it also be borne in mind that the hand of God
is ever upon the springs of the whole machinery,
and that what we only observe as fixity is in
reality His indefatigableness.   And then let it
be supposed that for us, His moral creatures,
He has a moral purpose to work out ; that He
is carrying on an inner moral plan here not
less important than His outer world-plan.   Why,
we ask, with all these conditions before us, is
it to be thought unlikely that, in furtherance of
such a plan, He should make Himself seen and
heard among men ?   The moral and intel-
lectual creature, man, has no inaptitude for
such a manifestation to him.   On the contrary,
if it has not really been made, then man has
imagined higher and more beautiful things—
nay, more morally ordered things—than have

yet been done for him. The course of nature properly understood furnishes no reason, we find, against such manifestation, for God has constantly changed His methods in nature, and God is always personally present in nature. According to our view, there can, in reality, be no such thing as Divine interference in nature; for the idea of interference pre-supposes a fixed incessant law which is broken in upon. There may, however, be, as we believe, no abstract law in nature at all, but an omnipresent Person, and that a Person who has repeatedly changed His natural processes. The only restriction we can really apply to His action is that it should be fit conduct under the circumstances. And we believe that the circumstances set out in Scripture are such as to make it fit for this present God to show Himself as present, and for Him who, while His purposes are unchanging, is yet ever so immensely fertile in changing method, to change His method here.

Indeed, the real question about God's showing Himself, as described in the Old Testament, and giving laws or working miracles,

must ever be not a question whether it is
possible, but whether it is likely. And the
more the matter is examined, the more it will
be found that there is not that strong prior
probability against such revelations which some
persons at first suppose. It will be our business
to show in the course of these pages that there
was, on the other hand, a very fit occasion
and strong call for such a course of conduct
being pursued; that the divine action in the
matter, as described in the Old Testament, is
not impulsive or fragmentary, but arranged
into harmonious and most appropriate combinations; that the same sort of orderly and
progressive advance is found there as in nature
itself; that there is a certain resemblance
between the revolutions in the one and in the
other; that there is the same incisive boldness
mixed with the same restrained economy of
resource in the general design; that the means
taken are justly fitted to the results professedly
aimed at; and that those results are in accordance with man's position and his prospects—
in short, that the Bible is a completion and
amplification of our best ideas of God; that it

accords with a comprehensive view of nature, with a knowledge of man's history, man's conduct, man's inner life, and not least that it applies itself fully to those fears and hopes in man which cannot otherwise be dispelled or satisfied.

CHAPTER II.

WHILE feeling bound to hold God to be the universal and absolute ruler in His whole creation, always and everywhere present, sustaining all things by the word of His power, and while looking on His ever-acting will as the incessant law in accordance with which all things live and move, we are compelled, at the same time, to make one exception to all this, and to hold that there is some degree of independence in the nature and conduct of men.

We must do this because we all feel and are convinced, without the necessity of any argument whatever, that we do possess some freedom of will and power of deciding for ourselves, and of either doing or leaving undone, in a vast variety of cases, as we may think fit. So that when we know, or believe we have ascertained, what is God's fixed will upon any subject, and what is right to be done, we may either conform our wills to it, or we may resist, and proceed in some opposite way of our own choice. It is perfectly clear to us, therefore, that we are not mere creatures of necessity, but that we do, in a certain sense, possess the liberty of choice in conduct commonly known as free-will.

And yet it is, at the same time, no doubt the case that, even though we cannot now be compelled to keep in the course of sound sense, prudence, justice, and piety, that this course is not the less good for us on that account. We may be able to act against the will of God now, but it is still good for us to keep the will of God now. For, since the whole world is sustained by His plan or present action, the only full and final meaning of good in it is agreement with Him or His plan, and the only full and final meaning of evil in it is disagreement with Him. That freedom, therefore, which enables us either to accept His ways or to reject them, while it is on one side a privilege, is, at the same time, on the other side, a responsibility also.

E

Nor is this responsibility a slight one. Indeed, the position of such frail and limited creatures as we certainly are, would be one of great risk were we endowed with this perilous sort of liberty, but left without any directions by which to keep ourselves straight in accordance with the course of the Divine government. It is not with us as with some other creatures. If we observe animals, we see that they are protected in this respect; for we find them by invariable processes, or by some invariable law inscribed in their nature, providing for their food, shelter, safety, rest, reproduction, and nurture of young; and those of them which live in communities we find always in steady allegiance to an unchanging sort of government and discipline. But we do not find any such equal constancy in the minds of men. On the contrary, so confused are our faculties, or so wayward is our will, that new movements of change may at any moment arise, and persons are to be met with, even in the most cultivated societies, who deny that there should exist such institutions as the home, or family, or property, or central government, and who refuse to accept any religion, or to believe in any God—in short, who, while they insist that man is nothing more himself than an animal, yet reject those natural methods or laws which animals are found partially observing.

It seems, then, that if we, who are thus unconstrained, were to be left to ourselves to discover by mere theory and experiments what might be the principles of God's will as to our affairs, our position would be worse than that of the lower animals, since, while our conduct ranges beyond instinct, our perceptions are not sufficiently clear and constant to enable us to keep with certainty to a course producing safety and happiness. Thus, then, there is a great and undoubted need for assistances and directions from the Divine Being, who has placed us here, if we are to know and abide in His way, and if our powers of moral choice, instead of becoming a snare, are to prove a blessing to us.

But now, if there are such wants as these, we may feel quite sure some provision is made in the Divine government to meet them. God's careful supplies for all other wants of His creatures make us feel confident He will not neglect us in this great one, if we really need help. And the reality of our need may be abundantly shown by such considerations of reason as have just been referred to.

And, indeed, is there not also in our general wide-spread belief that Divine communications are to be expected, and have been from time to time given, a very strong presumption on the matter? Do not these notions, even when rather visionary in form, yet all lead us towards one substantial and reasonable prospect? If it has always appeared to the mass of men likely and desirable that God should make known His will to us, and direct us in His ways, who can suppose that these impressions have been all unmeaning? If the children of men are so made and placed that they thus long to hear the Divine Father's voice, shall we undertake to say that He who has thus made and placed them has never spoken to them or intended to do so—that the affectionate desires of the creature can thus exceed the affectionate conduct of the Creator, and that we, usually so heavy in regard to spiritual things, have here the power of desiring more communion with Him than he has the intention or inclination of bestowing?

This would, indeed, be strange in so holy and beneficent a Being that He should place us in a position of want; that He should give or permit us a strong impression that our want would be supplied by Him ; and yet that, after all, here in that which seems best and nearest to His full mind and purpose, there should be a sudden break in His usual way of dealing; that requirements should now first no longer be balanced with supplies for them ; that difficulties should now first remain without remedy ; that there should at length be a cry from earth without an answering echo from Heaven. All this we cannot believe, for it would be contrary to the whole analogy of Providential dealings, which are constantly being enforced in the natural management of the world, that we should have a mission without instructions for its fulfilment, faculties without a field marked out for them, risks and responsibilities without provisions, so that they may be properly encountered. We must think it, then, on the whole, to be in the highest degree probable that, since we are furnished with these strong impressions about the Divine will, we are to expect, from some quarter or other, and in some way or other, a corresponding publication to us of that will.

But where, then, are we to look for this revelation? In what way has God directed us? Has He planted His law within us, or has He revealed it outwardly among us.

If it be only within us, as some affirm, what will be our position? Will it not, then, be the case that those universal impressions of the human heart which point to a distinctive and clear revelation have been really deceived? We shall have had a revelation, but so little expressive will it have been that we shall have all been going out at all times in search of another, unconscious that our want was already supplied, and, notwithstanding the supply, feeling the want still.

If an inner revelation leave us in such a state as this—if we can have it without so much as being aware of its existence, or being able to separate it from the movements of our natural faculties—the gift must, indeed, be in some degree illusory, and neither a fulfilment of our wishes in the matter, nor a complete supply for our wants. Supposing this all that had been done for us, it would be no wonder we should still be looking for something more, and be ready to regard with interest any external system seeming likely to give us more.

Take man even at his best—that is to say, under what we believe to be the dispensation of the Holy Spirit. Observe him when even thus highly endowed, and you will see into what excesses and aberrations he may still fall, unless the movements within are compared and harmonised with the law of religion outside. You will find that some of the saddest pages of Christian history are those which show how men who have believed themselves under so very full an inner light that they might venture to emancipate themselves from the outer legislation, have fallen into irregular and sometimes scandalous ways. The whole testimony of such experience is to the effect that the inner impressions of individuals are too liable to change, too dependent on various frames and circumstances, and too conflicting with one another to allow us to suppose them either to be the tablets on which the full law is written, or complete utterances of the law itself. Whatever may be done for us within, the results evidently require to be brought into contact with some external standard, if they are really to produce for us benefit or safety.

Once again, if we go to places where what we consider the right rule of conduct—that is, the rule founded on external law—has been shut out, and where evil habits—that is, an opposite rule—have long prevailed, there we shall find whole classes perfectly indifferent to our code of morality as to right and wrong, regarding us with hostility on account of it, and glorying themselves in what we consider their shame.

Again, take the case of children. We find in them that, though they have the power of responding readily to a rule of right and wrong, they yet invariably require to have it laid down for them from outside.

And, indeed, we must remember this, that if the law of right and wrong, instead of being in a measure external, were altogether let into

our very nature it might then become a question
whether we could ever do anything which
should not be in accordance with it—somewhat as it was said of old, that if it were part
of our nature to be virtuous, we could never
become vicious, as the stone, which naturally
falls downwards, can never be made to fall
upwards.* It might be a question too, whether,
even when men might differ extremely in their
notions of conduct, the notions of one side
might not have to be considered quite as valid
as those of the other, and whether we should
not have to suppose, not that there is one
inflexible moral will, but many various plans
for life, and that upon different natures the
Divine hand had written differences, something
like those we see in different sorts of animals,
giving to some the part of destroying, and to
others the part of being peaceable victims.
But such suppositions as these would come
near to be the end either of our moral freedom
or of God's moral order.

If, then, we allow that there are such qualities
in conduct as right and wrong, that these mean

* Aristot. Ethic.

C

what is in accordance or what is opposed to
God's will, that we have within us some faculty
which is capable of appreciating these differences and of being impressed by them, is it at
all likely, we ask, that God in making us thus
sensitive about them, and being Himself all
the time so interested for the sake of us and
all His creatures, the destinies of many of
whom are in our hands, that we should choose
right and avoid wrong, would yet leave it uncertain among us what right and wrong may
be.   Is it at all likely that He would, for
instance, make a conscience to approve and
condemn, and yet leave it to accident whether
it should approve or condemn in accordance
with His will or in opposition to it,—that He
would let it wander up and down to discover
or guess for itself, because He who has certainly
given us the faculty for advance, and certainly
seems to wish our advance, had yet neglected
to make known in any unmistakable way how
we ought to go forward.

We seem, then, by many considerations compelled to look for a law outside ourselves, and
we are reasonably impressed by the conviction

that God will not leave us unenlightened, but
that He will supply us with the clear direction
we need. We have seen that the mere movements of men together in society are far too
uncertain and fluctuating to be the means of
affording such aid as we are in search of,
and so we are brought to the conclusion that
it is very probable, and, indeed, we may say,
morally certain, that an outer revelation of
law has been given by God, and that the fact
which the Scriptures declare is in full accordance with what we are brought by reason
confidently to expect.

We accept it, then, to be commended as
essential that God has given us this outer
revelation of law, and now at this point a
very powerful concurrence of testimony unites
to show, with the strongest probability, that
this needed revelation is the one which is contained in the Bible.

For the law of the Bible has such qualities
as these. It so arranges its fundamental plan
as to fit in completely with the inner constitution of our nature. It applies itself fully to
deal with those social and religious discords

which we find from other sources were the most serious difficulties of the ancient world. It comes into the field attended by circumstances which, upon inspection, are found full of significance and propriety in themselves, and which are in full relation with the antecedent history. Its institutions, when professing to be moral, promulgate a morality which has never been superseded, and when arranging worship essentially accord with that which is still regarded as the highest religion. Even its civil and social regulations, though from their very nature charged with something which is but temporary, yet teem with principles and suggestions of continuing importance. The whole system is, further, not only complete in itself as an admirable and worthy method, but is associated in entire appropriateness with those long trains of development, extending over many centuries, brought in by various men under differing circumstances and in different places, which all together go to make up the Bible. And, finally, this ancient law, at last, joins in and mingles its stream with the living waters of the Gospel by which all modern society is fertilised, thus retaining the perpetual value which our Lord attributed to it, when He said that not one jot or tittle of it should pass away until all had been fulfilled, and which is a fitting quality of whatever has been solemnly revealed by God.*

These pretensions, wide though they may seem, are in reality but an imperfect statement of the claims of this admirable legal system, which the more one acquaints himself with its scope and details, will, we believe, the more commend itself to him as an essential basis of that general outer revelation of God to man, of which we are in search.

Indeed, if the study of Hebrew Law shows it really to possess these particular features of cohesion and fitness in any such degree as we attribute to it, then since an outer revelation has to be looked for, and can nowhere else be with any sufficiency supplied to us, it would be more strange that this one which was wanted, and which so exactly meets the want, should

---

* Aquinas, Summ. Theol. II. i. quæs. 91, and Augustin. de Lib. Arbit. 6.

not be divine than that it should be. If we find a locked door in the house, and, after trying all the other keys in vain, at length come to one which just fits and opens it, and which has no use anywhere else, we shall hardly be persuaded either that this one is not its key or that the door has no key at all.

These proprieties of the law, of which we have spoken, it will be our business successively to present, and to endeavour to show that to a fair and candid judgment they commend themselves as being not fictitious or forced, but as so substantial and real as to be worthy of the utmost consideration.

There may be points, as every one will be prepared to find, at which old familiar difficulties will rise on the surface, and to these their full weight should be given. At the same time we may fairly press this—that theology should be dealt with as all other subjects are by those who profess to regard theology as only on the same level with all other subjects—that is to say, that its evidences should be assorted and weighed as all other evidence is, and that we should not toss over the balance by any movement of prejudice, but keep steadily before our eyes the two scales to see after we have put in all we have to say for it on one side, and all we have to say against it on the other, which weighs the most.

If there are doctrines of Scripture which demand our faith they are attended by arrangements which address our reason. God, in claiming from us the submission of children, has offered us proof that such allegiance is worthy of our manhood, and it is a deplorable reply to the great appeals of the Bible to our intellect, when we form our conclusions about it with the quick partiality of the young, and only show the qualities of maturity in tenaciously clinging to our prejudices.

This very quickness with which some of us oppose and resent the details and idea of revelation is in itself a sign how much revelation is wanted, for if our inner state were really sound, what announcement would be hailed by us with such delight as this, that we are thus brought into a direct communication with the Author of all things, and that God Himself

has not thought it unfit to visit personally the
sons of men.   And if our reasoning faculties
were really well pointed, on what subject
should we exercise them more persistently and
more lovingly than on this one?   How difficult
it would be to take from us our convictions
about it.   How ingeniously we should exercise
ourselves in exploring it.   What immense
stores of proof we should accumulate.   With
what ardour should we resist aggressions.
How despondent we should be when our
prospect seemed to be overcast, and how
happy it would make us when the clouds
seemed to be moving off.

A world whose general experience is the
reverse of this—which is ardent and ingenious on many subjects, but indifferent and
dull on the greatest one of all, which asserts
its importance, while it turns away from that
which would really show it important—which
is credulous enough in other matters, but
sceptical in the one where it should most
incline to belief—which refuses to accept on
trust, and will not take the trouble to convince
itself by examination—such a world, we must

think, whatever may be said of it in other respects, is certainly one which by wisdom knows not God, and which, therefore, requires that God should in mercy make Himself known to it.

Our conclusion, then, upon the whole subject of an outer revelation of law is this: taking into account the disinclination of our tastes and the ingenuity of our mental powers, our responsible position as the highest creatures on earth, a sort of vicegerents over other beings for God, the needfulness of direction in it, and our tendency and aptitude for receiving directions by the way of law, and also our general desire and expectation that some such communication would be given,—taking all these things into account, we cannot suppose that nothing of the sort has been done, and that all this darkness, thundering, smoke, and trumpet-sound in the moral sphere is accompanied by no speaking voice whatever.

Further, we cannot suppose it likely that the revelation of law would be given merely in an internal way, in which it would interfere

with our independence and with our responsibilities, and be complicated with our natural
faculties, and be undiscernible with certainty
as the Divine voice, bringing up constantly
such questions as what utterances are human
and optional, what Divine and compulsory,
and which one of the many conflicting systems
might be from God, and which of the parts
in that one, conflicting among themselves,
might be from Him.

We are further unable to suppose this from
noting the uncertainty of our judgments,
which often make wrong decisions, and still
more of our affections, which often fix on
unworthy objects and run in unworthy
courses, all which seems to show that no
such distinctly-revealed internal law does, in
fact, reside in us. So, too, does the observation of children, who have at first to receive
rules from outside, though then very readily
applying them, and of vicious societies, which
have some rules quite contrary to the laws of
right elsewhere—as, for instance, the rule of
hereditary revenge.

So that, on the whole, when an outer law

so well fits our faculties, and tends to so much benefit, and obviates so many objections, and answers to so strong a presentiment, we may very fully believe that it is in this way we have indeed been legislated for by God, who, having placed us in a world of natural law which is outwardly apparent to us, and of social law, which is also outwardly enacted for us, and who, having permitted desires within us for something of the like sort from Him, and given us such a sense of happiness and security in feeling that He has bestowed it, has evidently no necessary disapproval of the application of such a method in our case.

And, lastly, when the Bible law professing to be from God has so many qualities which commend it to our sense of fitness and right, and has been so useful both in religion and indirectly, but widely, in society also; while it still shows itself full of vitality and meaning, and yet promises to have even more extensive fields of usefulness and more complete practical successes in the future; when it is guaranteed to us by such a vast cloud of witnesses and by such varied methods of testimony, it is not unreasonable but the reverse to conclude this to be the revelation we are in search of, and the required legislative machine for carrying out the divine government of mankind.

CHAPTER III.

ONENESS of origin in the human race is a theory now commonly accepted. An opponent of religion would gain little by denying it. There are such essential points of resemblance between nations the most remote that if we supposed these distinct in origin we should only have new difficulties to account for.

Those who go back step by step through different methods of government, and note their relationship and rise one out of another, are at last, as by a sort of necessity, brought to a single tribe as the original social unit, and from that to a single family as the root of the tribe. Supposing ourselves in presence of such an original primeval family, however rude, we should surely find that a natural order, known even among animals, would make the parent its chief. He it would be

who would provide and protect, and his
power and affection would impress those
under him. This is no assumption. It is
observable everywhere in nature, even in dens
and nests.

Among beings of long minority, and capable
of retaining and recording impressions, we
may be sure corresponding ideas of reverence
and allegiance would be attracted, and accumulate round this natural chief. As regards
religion, even supposing it only earth-born,
the parent, we might safely presume, would
be its first mover and representative. But if
it be allowed that God has at any time com-
municated with our race in a direct and immediate way, then that communication, we may
be sure, would begin with the parent. The
great Parent would, we may be sure, respect
and accredit the human parent's position.
The offspring, on the other hand, would
readily respect the human parent's announcements. In any case, then, religion would be
cast in the paternal form. But though the
children might be prone to adopt this, why,
unless it were true, should the parent be

inclined to put such a religion forth? What interest has one practically supreme to transfer his supremacy to another? What suggestions could move one really isolated to feign himself in close dependence? If he was a coward through inexperience, the strange sights around might teach him many things, but why this—that he had a father-god? How could the first parent have understood and felt a parent never speaking, never coming? If it be said vividness of imagination filled the void, then how came a true want asking for supply to be satisfied with an untruth, and why, in a real nature, was this flagrant unreality written? However ingeniously the notion may be laboured, a really probable theory against revelation can hardly be framed; and we may reasonably hold it as fact that a primeval revelation was made to men.

There is, further, nothing improbable in the circumstance of revelation having paternal features. The first dealings with children in every home are far more immediate and condescending than at later periods of their life.

It is still necessary that the first lessons should
be learnt from mouth and hand.   Why, then,
when there were no documents, no traditions,
no society, and yet a first man to be taught
and a machinery to be set going—why should
we say, " No, it is fitter that God should keep
back and not speak at all than that he should
so speak.   The universal credulity which believed it otherwise was an universal mistake
of men as to what they wanted.   The universal tradition which recorded it as fact was
an universal deception as to what had taken
place ?"

Those, indeed, seem but inconsistent advocates of humanity who, while on one side they
deny our fall, on the other thus deny our
aspirations.   Far more reasonable is that
position which asserts a gradual development
of man, retarded but progressive, opposed yet
rising through defeats, and the whole movement divisible at last by a three-fold crisis of
demarcation, supported at each point by its
special appropriate guarantee of miraculous
manifestation, viz., moral individualism under
the Messiah ; social constitutionalism by means

of Moses; domesticity from God to the patriarchal parent.

We suppose then the primeval home to be the original bed from which religion, law, sociology first grew. We suppose each of these to represent human thought, feeling, and circumstance, springing, changing, fading, and springing again over ever-increasing areas of growth under the influences of the world and of heaven. The family, society, law, as well as religion itself, are in this sense connected with the divine, and will all proceed by principles and methods having some analogy and relation. Further, if such a view be correct, no institutions of law, society, or religion, inconsistent with the original family frame will be likely to win permanent success. This seems strongly corroborated by experience. It is also strongly insisted on in the religion of Jesus. The family idea is at the very root of all our Saviour's teaching. That idea in its widest applications was antagonistic to the sentiment of his hearers. To them it disparaged his claims; to a truer philosophy it most highly commends them.

But now if there was thus oneness of origin in man ; if the family was the first social unit and the parent the first social power, and the first depository and propagator of divine communications—if, in accordance with the documentary teachings of religion, the home was the centre from which first came law, society, and religion, let us see if we can trace in any probable way the advancing move-ment.

First, it would seem clear that as by the side of the original chief and father there grew up his sons, themselves the centres of families of their own, so by the side of the will and interests of the first tent there would stand out the will and interests of the other tents which surrounded it. The body of questions rising, and moved in this way, would by degrees arrange themselves into the uncon-scious beginnings of system. This would supply one side of rudimentary law, which would come into form through the counterplay of interest and affection, independence and allegiance. The other side of it, if other side we allow, would pass by means of the parent from the divine Providence ruling over man and over man's institutional and personal movements.

We suppose then human society as originally a family, and afterwards as a tribe with interests gradually forming, experience gradually accumulating, questions gradually arising and all receiving settlements which gradually took force as customs. But we imagine as engaged in this work not only the will, reason, and impulses of the offspring, but also those of the parent; and further, and besides both, acting over all through the parent for the benefit of the general body, in some way appropriate to the time, we imagine, the divine Author and Parent of this infant society.

We suppose, for instance, that the Altar was a real meeting point between earth and heaven, and not a mere arrangement of stones ; a place where the conscience went to speak, that it might listen and hear echoes of itself. And we suppose, too, that there was thus from the first a divine element in human affairs twisted in among the conclusions of policy as a gift from heaven itself, a vantage point for further combinations in after times as further messages might descend from heaven.

We suppose, also, that to some extent, in consequence of the position of the early chiefs between the human and divine, these came to be regarded not only with filial allegiance but also with religious reverence, and that the one man thus highly designated and set apart began to originate that idea and mental frame which gradually produced world governors, and which sometimes, when light was lost sight of, ended in depravation by attributing to these divine honours.

Patriarchal longevity must have tended to concentrate and economise the divine action in revelation, and to accumulate rapidly and effectually the experiences of the race, but if we advance our stand to a period when life was shortened, population extended, and migrations constant, then the patriarchal system would be on the wane. Its outer appearance might be retained as a social theory, as was the case, for instance, at Rome at a much later period, but its old beneficent character would, as there, have left it; and its methods, deprived of their early meaning, would lean to oppression.

At such a period as this there would commence, and gradually advance, the unconscious struggle to disentangle the idea of individual rights from the patriarchal custom. Simple as this work appears to us who look back, still it was no doubt attended with great difficulties at the time; the very idea of social individualism seems to have been in some sense strange to the early world. Property and even life itself were regarded as belonging to the tribal community. Injuries to either one or the other were looked on mainly as losses to the tribe, and theirs it was to claim retribution or recompense.

The rights of persons, as elaborated by our own law, almost self-evident as they may in many points now seem, in fact, represent a long train of legal triumphs, and are the joint result of several contributing causes. Among these the law of Moses has fulfilled an important function. Hardly any other system bound together its community with so much stringency as his into an organic whole. In none other does the entire plan recognise and bring out each individual in such emphatic manner. The liberality of its general privilege embraces the community, but within that wide machinery there is again an active lesser wheel of personal responsibility and communion. The covenant is with Israel at large, but the " thou " of the commandment and the offerer's hand on the victim intimate that the law was already taking up the ground requisite for the great achievements of the gospel.

The " natural system " of society as we may name it would, of course, have to pass through many modifications of arrangement and many phases of development in proportion as refinements in relationship grew up in advancing communities. We cannot suppose, however, that the original ground-idea of that first system could ever be well modified or departed from, and for this reason—it embodies the truths that a common origin and tie of natural connexion bind us all together; that there are primary interests common to us all ; that there are certain benefits and losses which, while only partial, perhaps, in incidence, are yet universal in result, and that though men and communities absorbed in the particular parts assigned to them may fail to observe the fact, yet that there is one drama of history which has been continuously playing out, that its whole cast is based upon the domestic idea, and that our common phrase " the human family " is by no means a figure of speech, but has a substantial and very meaning truth in it.

Indeed, if we regard society as presided over by the one heavenly Author, we cannot suppose it likely that the original sentiment of its order would ever be abandoned by Him. That sentiment was not arbitrary but natural, that is, it was essentially connected with his continuous world-plan, and consisted in this principle, that men should be combined by the impulse and tie of the affections which flourish in family relationship. As societies have increased in size the affections have retreated into the private home, and concentrated themselves there, but we cannot think that God, having once impressed on the whole order of our affairs this highest moral method and principle, would ever abandon it, and consent to have the compul-

sions of mere rule substituted in its stead.
We may feel reasonably confident, as a matter
of probability, that the first donation expressed
the permanent design ; that the family idea has
still existence and meaning for society, and
that it will gradually be worked out in public
affairs so as to conform our present organisations of expediency and partial benevolence
to the original sentiments of our nature, by
this means solving many of the great social
problems of modern life and promoting to the
utmost the general good.

But observe, if this be so, what a testimony
is already supplied in favour of Hebrew law,
for that which consideration leads us to expect
is just what this system has already set to work
to bring about. It collects together a nation
under the express theory of its being a family,
legislating for it as for children of a common
father, and bringing its enactments constantly
to the test of fraternal duty and regard. This
idea is never abandoned throughout the whole
law or the whole Scripture. It is enforced
with even increased urgency in the prophetic
writings, and forms one of the main features

in the Gospel, where indeed it is expanded to vast proportions, the affections being regarded as the substantive power of the law, the whole world-wide society of Christians being looked on as one great brotherhood, God Himself distinctly taking the title of "Father," and the Son of God that of "Brother," and the dimensions of the plan extending themselves so as to incorporate by adoption the human society into a far larger family organisation and "general assembly" of other beings besides us who are on earth ; a glimpse being thus afforded us of the probability that the whole government and dealing with this world is an harmonious part of a much wider and perhaps universal plan.

But now if we return and think again of many elements of difficulty and disturbance which may probably have surrounded early society, we may well imagine that on the relaxation of the patriarchal idea the new individualised life, before achieving rights, would in most communities have to pass through a long series of restraints. There is abundant evidence that such was indeed the case, and that the early modifications of the patriarchal

I

system were not immediately productive of
individual happiness or liberty.

Indeed it is clear that the breaking up of so
beautiful a central idea as that of the family
system, unless it could have been at once sup-
plemented by some other system equally compulsory on the affections, could hardly prove for
the immediate common good. No such other
system, however, was ready. The methods
which came on repeated the incidents of what
had gone before. There was the one ruler whose
word was still law. The people, however
graduated in rank among themselves, were in
relation to him regarded as all equal in dependence. "Patriarchal economy" still furnished the type. One predominant character
still formed a centre, and all the rest were in
equal subordination around. This method was,
according to Aristotle,* reflected in all the
oldest governments, which copied the features
of the family plan. Republics and other free
forms were the result of later art and refinement.

Such empires spread themselves as their

* I. Polit.

armies advanced, and often contracted again as they retreated. Their parts were cemented together by no moral principle touching the affections. Homage and tribute was what they required, for these brought provinces within their circle. As a result they were narrowed or overturned with a rapidity equal to their rise. Their foundations were not deeper than those of an old tribal encampment. It needed but a revolt, defeat, death, or palace intrigue, and it was as if the tents had been struck in a single night.

Such false patriarchalism was merely mimetic. Without customary rights founded on the idea of brotherhood, it was deprived of the spirit of the old law, and thus, though it was the birth of nationalism, it was a birth among terrible throes, in which family, property, and life all suffered. It was antithetical, indeed, to the older parental sentiment. It was the adumbration of an inner world-power tyrannical and injurious. The old oriental empires, though a political advance and a step in organisation, were a moral decline as weakening the highest motive principle for mankind, viz.,

that of a common tie in feeling, and weakening, together with that, the vigour of domestic
relations and social law.

The tenacious methods of thought of the
older time would, on the arrival at this stage,
be in some respects even disadvantageous.
The strong feeling of relationship, for instance,
would become the strong feeling of nationalism,
and would retard advance by rendering the
incorporation of new elements on equal terms
more difficult, setting up feudatory arrangements, and depressing the populations most
recently added.

The same family impulses tending to con-
strain men within hereditary callings would
bring out the features, and by degrees the entire system, of caste. Among these social sub-
divisions the bodies conversant with religion
and war would, from the prominence of their
professions, soon stand out and take the lead.
But what would be the result? War, once
made the interest of a class, would become
systematic. Religion committed to a sect would
be overlaid with accumulations of legend, and
symbolised into excess. It is at this point that

the political chief would be in danger of gradually developing into a power at once hostile to the authority of God and to the progress of society.

Let loose from the restraint of a moral rule enforced by sacred sanctions of religion, traditions of affection, and deep tribal sympathies, it is evident that the strong would begin to assert themselves more unrestrainedly, and that the weak would begin to suffer in proportion. Adventurous and gifted men would substitute personal merit for rank in the family as the ground of chieftainship, and the society, passing beyond the limits of the gens or clan, would be extended as far as the capacities and achievements of the ruler would permit.

Such a condition may have been an approach to social advance, but would be one attended with drawbacks, for after the original patriarchal tie had once been broken through, it might take long' to reconstruct the delicate machinery of a fresh moral claim on behalf of the weak against the strong, of a fresh public opinion for its support, of a fresh positive law to define its shape, and a fresh central authority to sustain its activity.

In the absence of all this, or prior to it, we should have to expect social disorder, such as uprisings of the oppressed, inroads upon personal security, and upon morals and property, and also a gradual exaggeration of patriarchal phenomena: the subjugation of the weak, children kept severely under power, women restrained into seclusion, and the mass of men brought into servitude. And such, in fact, is usually found as the condition of the ancient post-patriarchal world, and of those modern societies which may still be seen in something like that state of transition. Here, in short, would be patriarchal methods, but without the patriarchal spirit. Family subjection untempered by family affection. Absolutism of position with no limitations from feeling; the husks of the past preparing the soil of the future.

On reviewing the whole ground of the question, then, it may appear very natural that a difficulty should have presented itself to writers like Aristotle, while observing the vast influence of individual chiefs, in understanding how this could have arisen and been sustained. Such a writer could not easily suppose personal pre-eminence universal enough to account for it. The idea of supernatural sanctions as its support had come down to his days enfolded in such distorted legends that it was not often seriously dealt with by philosophy.

The question which embarrassed him still remains to be met. If the chief of the later or poetic age were merely an heroic " Basileus," chief by his merit in war and in council, his position would be simple and easy to be understood; but mixed in with these qualities there are found numerous traces both of family headship and allegiance, and also of religious functions and prerogatives, all attached to his office or person. This throws us back at once upon the remoter patriarchal system, and we have to suppose its prior existence as described in Scripture as the foundation and cause of these peculiarities in later society.

Some persons, perhaps unwilling to allow this explanation, have recently attempted to account for these phenomena by affirming as

something certain that in the infancy of mankind there was no conception at all of law as a
system or set of rules endued with a continuing
force, but that every law was conceived of as
a separate inspiration from above given to the
tribe through the chief; that there was no
power in men's minds of dividing religion,
morals, and legislation into distinct topics, according to our present ways of regarding them,
but that these subjects were all mixed up together in the mind; that there were hardly
even customs existing in connection with them,
but that when emergency called them out they
were regarded as emanations for the occasion
which descended from above, and that in this
way the special dignity and pre-eminence of
chiefs first came to be believed in.

But assuming these statements (though difficult perhaps of exact proof) to have been
quite accurately made, we are at once struck
with the following inference : how completely
this theory brings us — where its authors
may not intend — within the range of the
books of the Pentateuch, and how far more
naturally and probably the narrative of that

part of Scripture accounts for the ancient condition of the social world than do the surmises
intended to supplant it. If the mind of man
in its earlier stages was thus weak in power;
unable by itself to frame rules of action in such
a way as to be impressive; what more likely
than that the Divine Author should give it the
needed help; that He should come to it again
and again with a command in great matters
delivered to its venerated leaders, and so impress them and enable them to impress others,
and that then afterwards, when habits of
thought were formed, and accumulations of
experience made, He should gradually withdraw from this immediate action, and out of
respect for our freedom veil Himself, as we
find He does at present. Such a supposition
would afford at once a sufficient ground for expecting just such Divine dealings as Scripture
describes to us as having actually taken place.

And further, suppose it the case that in
those earliest times religion, social government, and morals were mixed in with law, is
that an infirmity or defect? Is it not rather
just the high character and tone which law

K

would take while a Divine Power was moving
immediately among its arrangements ; a pre-
monition of that which we hope for as the
future ideal when the Will of God immediately
present and unreservedly accepted shall introduce a personal divine rule and a direct worship, which together shall bind up in a perfect
polity both the social, mental, and religious
man.

Nor indeed are we to take it too readily for
granted that the sharp distinctions supposed
between modern law, religion, and morals
exist always in more than a technical way, or
that where they are really admitted they
represent an improvement and advance instead of a decline in man's position.   Surely it
is not anything to boast of that a community
can regulate its action in one of such points
without reference to the rest of them;   and
surely any mental conception and treatment of
one of these subjects without regard to the
bearings of the rest can hardly be regarded
as comprehensive and complete.

We conclude, then, generally that the ancient patriarch as an original mover of law

presents to us the mental point of departure of the whole system of society—reverence for an authority based upon affection, and supported by divine communications; regard for life, domestic ties, property, and good name, as all within the circle of which the one revered family head was the centre, and over which the unseen Divinity was wielding his sanctions. The succeeding depravations show us the heart and life withdrawn from this old system, and its external forms consequently aggravated by the corruption of their very beauty, and forced into all the more unsightly and harder methods of tyranny.

At this point the Law of Moses came in to accept and appropriate all the ground made good by advancing civilisation, but to reject its errors, and to plant again all those early principles which were fading or dying out; to emphasise with the authority of Jehovah the duties and affections which spring from the family source, and, by grouping all together round the idea of home, to ingrain into the very soil of society the foundation thought of love.

The commandments of Sinai are thus not mere abrupt and fragmentary utterances. They are the complement of the earliest good estate of the world, the recipe for its later corruptions, the line upon which its advancing course is to run, and the significant forecast of its completest future. The fatherhood once more brought into the ascendant does not indeed recover its political position, but it gives us glimpses of its still more splendid expansion in the coming fatherhood of the future, while from this there depend the graces of fraternal society represented in the rules of the law as to love, purity, justice, truth, and absence of self-seeking; graces, whose notes, examplars, exercise, and abandonments are illustrated in the earliest Mosaic record; then distinctly thrown into the form of command; then, again, seen gradually vindicating themselves in history, until they find their full ratification in the teaching and conduct of Jesus, and after him their ever widening sphere in the Church of the Spirit, which he founded, so that these principles are now the safeguards of society, the constant antagonists of all forces which would fetter its energies, disturb its progress, and corrupt its tone, and thus the gradual preparers of the final condition when the matured life shall have at length realised in the highest degree those relationships which it at first knew of but in shadows and lesser forms.

Lastly, then, we may emphasise this observation that in the theory of society which revelation puts forward, we find progress secured by just the same sort of counterplay between contending principles of good and evil which are found at work in the actual world. We have, that is, depressions of the great patriarchal idea so morally dignified and so fit to be the first gift brought out of Paradise. We have those depressions as effects partly of social, but mainly of moral changes, and we have in them by the side of certain advantages, such as a more organised and ductile polity, proportionate difficulties, a paling and a falling away, for instance, of the filial brotherly and paternal sentiments which were and always must be among the most cogent which can exist among us. We find the whole series of family ideas and incidents prevailing in appearance in the oriental despotism, but lowered in tone and value; and then we have in the crisis of the Hebrew commonwealth an appropriation of all the best results of this strong civil rule, but a new reinvigoration of the whole with the family spirit.

We venture to think that the foundation of this Hebrew state thus presents a central point in sociology. The fusion of the family of Abraham with a selection of Egyptian methods was the junction of the highest phase of patriarchal life with the best parts of monarchism. The Hebrews had shown the extent of their development by the tenacity of their isolation. The vigour of the principles which animated them may best be estimated by their long-continued resistance and power of rebound. They had that immense vitality which is still found in a degree among tribes kept together by the patriarchal feeling.

The Hebrew, even independent of his spiritual uses, was perhaps the best conceivable vehicle for restoring or continuing this great principle of society. In the Hebrew State the family spirit budded once more. Through the

vicissitudes of that State in connection with
Egypt, Babylon, the Greeks, and Rome, the
whole mass of civilisation became gradually
prepared to receive this principle in the strong
way in which Christianity was at length to
endorse it. What was at first a family nation had
already under the Hebrew kings become a family
of the religious within a nation. This had been
the work of the prophets. In the Gospel the
religious were finally advanced to be a family
within all nations. All the world was to be a
brotherhood, but with individual rights and
responsibilities fully recognised, for each nation
also was to be in a certain sense a fatherhood.

The influence of Christianity wherever it has
prevailed has restored to governments, no
matter what their outer form, something of the
spirit which breathed in the original tent life.
Though the main leader is no longer the
human ruler, but the divine, the human chief is
respected as the vicegerent of heaven, and
social relationships are impressed again with
the beginnings of family regard.

Wherever, on the other hand, Christianity
has been comparatively unsuccessful through
defective methods of presentment, or through

an express rejection by the influences of society, there have been again exhibited those turbulences, revolutions, and class animosities which were so frequent in the ancient imperial world.

Revelation, then, we have to regard not merely as religious, but as governmental; as the union of man with the moral Governor not merely for the future, but for the present as well; not merely to secure us for the coming life, but also for that which now is.   The system of Moses we regard not as something which may be accepted or let alone, but as an essential constituent of the original whole, necessary not only for the development of religion, but for the advance of society as well, and precious in our civil liberties and happiness as it is in our spiritual condition and prosperity.   We are constrained, therefore, to think, without now speaking of the soul, those persons sadly infatuated who, having any of this world's benefits to lose either for themselves or their families, conspire to weaken by indifference or opposition orthodox religious convictions which there is so much reason to believe to be the preserving salt of society, as well as the seeds for heaven.

CHAPTER IV.

THERE has been, both in the order of society itself and also of its two guides, law and religion, a course of development somewhat similar in kind. Society beginning in the home passes through the period of tyranny, and advances to responsible government; law beginning at expressions of paternal will, hardens into custom, from which it by degrees emerges into adapted legislation; religion first bowing to revelations at the patriarchal altar, afterwards prostrates itself, as we shall presently find, before the departed patriarch himself, but at last rises to direct communications with the Divine. In each of these spheres we seem to have the preliminary position of an infant community, the aberration of its early advance, and then its final settlement in the higher station.

The history of civilisation is thus an outward

epitomised expression of the complete destiny of the race; that is, of a childhood infantile under God, a youth slavish under sin, and a maturity manly in the Church of the first-born. The Mosaic history again expresses in a still more condensed form the same progression: the family state under Jacob, the servile under Pharaoh, the free under Moses— a serial arrangement which is appropriate, since that history has been a special agency by means of which the advance of mankind has been carried forward. Thus, then, revealed religion, truly understood, is not a something rigid and archaic, reared up by the side of civil life and social advance, distinct from and indifferent to them, but it is the seed, and soul, and spring—the very life-blood, nerve, and muscle of all that is vital and valuable in our affairs, from which there surely comes, and to which there may probably be traced, what is really true and good in them.

But before showing the workings of the Law of Moses in this respect, we should go on from the decline of the patriarchal state into tyrannies, to note the decline of the patriarchal religion into idolatries; that is to say, before describing the return, we should complete our account of the wandering away.

Though increase and movement of population would be one cause of the break up of the patriarchal system, the severe and sudden convulsions attending the change seem to show wide-spread moral corruption as a further cause. There may have been pressure on the part of tribe-leaders, but before this there must have been some solicitation of pressure by the tribes. When peoples are enslaved, they are themselves usually forgers of the chain. The tyrannies which desolate their life are but the recoil of their own follies and offending.

The one primeval altar may probably have been designed as the basis to support the one parental centre of social unity in the early world, even as the tabernacle or temple afterwards became the central institution to keep up the national integrity of the descendants of Abraham. The disruption from the primeval family would tend to cause schism from the patriarchal altar, as it did afterwards

in the divided kingdoms of Judah and Israel.
In the new societies, involved often in attacks
on the life and property of their neighbours,
religion, already separated from its centre,
would soon further decline.   The faith of a
community will not remain far in advance of
its morals, and a national career essentially
untrue would by degrees tinge early religion
with its falsehoods.   The lowest point of
worship reached by them, in which imaginary
deities, themselves reputed criminal, were pro-
pitiated by criminal acts of their votaries,
expressed the extremest departure not only
from the ancient patriarchal faith, but also
from its morality.

We may now go on to observe how, human
passions having usurped the place of divine
law, human personality substituted itself for
divine fatherhood, underneath which, since
the passions dominating society were evil, the
author of evil came to be the " prince of this
world ; " the tyrannies which were rampant in
it being his tyranny ; the worship which was
offered in it becoming a sacrifice to devils.

There was, doubtless, much in the ancient

chief to impress the imagination of early society. Even apart from Scripture, we have evidence that his authority was final, and that his position was considered almost sacred. His judgments were respected as in some measure divine, and his person regarded with a reverence approaching to worship. Traces of this ancient idea are found extending even far on in history. Thus Strabo comments on the almost divine honour (σεβασμὸs θεοπρεπὴs) with which the Persian kings were regarded by their subjects, a habit which he holds to have been derived by them from the more ancient Aryan Medes.* By some mysterious link these sacred leaders, heads of religion and of law, appeared to their people to unite them to the unseen.

Now, imagine the decline and death of a great chief of immense age; long eminent for courage, endurance, wisdom, and piety; long regarded with the utmost reverence and affection; the depositary of ancient traditions; associated with the forefathers of the world; himself a central agency in religion and law;

---

* Strabo, 'Geog.' 525.

the medium of intercourse with the spiritual
sphere ; the offerer of sacrifice; the dispenser
and, as it might seem, the procurer of blessings;
the great guide and guardian; the authority
as to the relationships of life and business.
When such a personage might be at length
taken away after a very long career, nothing
would be more easy than for the minds of his
followers, feeble and leaning towards supports,
to imagine him still watching over them, and
hovering around ; to remember him in stated
festivals, and to carry on rites of reminiscence
in his honour.   By degrees, as the memory of
this chief's earthly residence became dim, these
impressions as to his superior life, his continued interest, patronage, and mediation in
their behalf, might well grow in intensity, and,
if true religious faith were weak, from com-
memoration there would inevitably come the
risk of passing to a species of cultus.   There
is a widely-spread impression that such a
cultus of ancestors was, if not the only, at any
rate one of the chief doors by which idolatry
entered the world.   The degree of tendency
in the ancient mind towards such an attitude

may be gathered from observing the immense importance attached to funeral rites. To have died without them was regarded as a greater calamity than death; to have failed to perform them as only a lesser misfortune.

When once the matter had got so far, the remaining steps could be taken only too easily. The association of the ancestor to be honoured with some natural object commensurate with his dignity, or connected with his life or person, is but the symbolism of an almost instinctive heraldry. From this to the construction of figures, either directly or typically representative, is again only one further, and not less natural, movement.

But to dwell on this transition a little more in detail. We have the following complication of motives moving around this matter, of such vital importance to the condition of the ancient world:—a rapid growth of society to proportions beyond the reach of patriarchal arrangements; movement of locality resulting, which would still further increase the inadequacy of those arrangements; conflict among unsettled marauders as a consequence; these in their

turn leading to aggregations round gifted
leaders; the raising of such leaders by degrees
into the position of Oriental despots, invested
in the popular esteem with the patriarchal
prestige, that is, with authority of the most
sacred compulsion; yet leaders too recent in
elevation, too near at hand in administration,
too precarious in position, too unfit in themselves, and also for the most part too much
checked in religion by a hierarchy developing
itself by the side of their own power to
be able to minister to spiritual wants and
aspirations of a people accustomed to lean
upon the venerable and pacific majesty of
the primeval fathers, and to regard them
as the intermediary channels with the Divine.

Indeed, however much we suppose revelation weakened in its influence over the ancient
populations, or however little we allow as a
probability that it was in fact a donation
to them from heaven, we may still see that
the ancient despot, owing to something essentially untrue in his position, could not really
supply the place of the patriarch in religion.
That interrelation of interests which in the

patriarchal polity had flourished among the traditions of parents and descendants was in the tyranny no longer fostered. Another theory of lord and subject was now suggested, or rather impressed upon the new communities, through the exigency of the military events to which they owed their origin and maintenance. The absolute authority and unquestioning subjection generated in camps were features of these States, in some respects little more than encampments themselves.

Under such a condition of things the old ideas and methods of thought, too deeply rooted to be at once removed, would be pressed into a new form. In popular esteem the paternal attributes would still in a measure cling to the person of the despot, and, to some extent, the supernatural relations of the Patriarch would also be attributed to him. This treatment lingered so long that, even where a priestly caste had been developed, the despot was, on ascending the throne, admitted into it. But his position was in reality without the family sanction. The rights of the home and of property, the rights of life and death,

M

of personal liberty and equitable decision, were during his presidency all in a transition state. A new diploma and authority was now wanted to give, on the one hand, moral force to the Governor, and on the other hand to restrain his individual will which without this would be entirely absolute, or only limited on certain sides by custom, or by sectional restraints distinct from the general interest.

This inadequacy was still greater in religion. In the simple circle of the patriarchal tents had been a real temple, or sacred enclosure, more distinct than if marked by Druid stones, and within which moral principles, family affections, social rights and duties, had found their first nidus and nursing place, and had come, through the instrumentality of the Patriarch, into direct contact with the spiritual, and with that great unseen Power, the Father of the fathers.

Here, by the side of social progress, had expanded the religious elementary principles of faith, the religious affection of love and reverence, and the religious duties of obedience. Here the first outline of the future, as fulfilled for us by the Holy Spirit and the Son of God, had been mysteriously traced in Divine whispers, and mysteriously embodied for use in the religion of sacrifice. The earliest supply for the essential wants of man had thus been provided. A rule had developed itself for right conduct, a remedy for errors. But the despot could no longer fulfil these functions; a line of separation therefore began to be traced, and the popular mind sought to retain its religious treasures by clinging to the past. It was at this point the Patriarch would become idealised. The veneration for ancestors who had been long known as the medium with the Divine, and as the traditional heroes of the race, now served as the stepping-stone to a new religious cycle, destined gradually to obscure the simple traditional worship and revealed hopes and realities which had been handed down from the beginning; leading to many and extreme exaggerations of worship and belief in corrupted communities, but after a time gradually to decline before a higher development of the first patriarchal faith, towards whose spread these very defects may in some inscrutable way have tended.

The track of this transition from the patriarchal to the idolatrous is traceable in a sufficiently probable way in some mythologies of the early world. It is usually found in these that they have one feature or representative of divinity rising above the rest. This divinity commonly appears in the dual form, as male and female, a great father and a great mother. At times, however, the conception is condensed into a quasi-unity; at other times it is still further simplified into a complete unity. In this divinity, in whatever way conceived, there is further observed a tendency to a twofold manifestation. He appears bearing the traces of two distinct pairs or personages in two succeeding avatars. Below the first group of the great father and the great mother there again ranges a high though subordinate series in the form of a triad of gods and associated goddesses.

In connection with this whole system there often occurs the idea of a creative germ floating on an abyss, and of an ark resting upon waters.

These sometimes have only a cosmical value, at other times they rise until they become equivalent to the great mother. A mountain is also a very usual feature in these systems, as a home of the gods and seat of the blessed.

All the above features in the mythological systems are so generally reproduced, and attended at times with such striking similarities in detail, that if we are permitted to start from the theory already referred to, that the idolatries of the old world were based on the reverence of ancestors, the outlines of patriarchal history at once offer themselves, giving us in a very natural way the key to the whole development. The great father and the great mother in their repeated forms will under such a treatment be the first parents Adam and Eve, and will afterwards be more distinctly the second parents, Noah and his wife. The triads connected with them will be the three sons of Adam and their wives, and then the three sons of Noah and their wives.

Besides the great persons, the great events, creation and deluge, paradise, the first donation of land, and the restoration of the land after the deluge, will be pointed at; while interwoven with these will be traces of heavenly manifestation and a divine unity and fatherhood, remnants of a higher truth, blending with allegories of the birthplace of Eden and the exit from the ark, imagined sometimes as the first mother.

We find in the mythologies a mountain, especially a three-peaked mountain, suggestive of Ararat, selected as the sacred spot. And in low countries we have artificial elevations, as mounds, pyramids, or towers, raised for religious rites. We also have an ark, sometimes as a cist, sometimes as a boat, the constant and prominent feature of such worships.

In the popular and religious theories and also in the mysteries there may further be traced two succeeding phases of idea, analogous to the periods before and after the deluge, the one of depression and disturbance preceding a religious crisis, the other of joy and prosperity following on it. With the former set of ideas we find associated the terrors and cruelties of heathen worship; with the latter, its sensual licence and riotous indulgence. This crisis, too, was frequently marked in the rites by a passage through water. All these features tend to show how probable it is that the ancient Scriptural fathers of the human race, and the great events among which they moved, were impressed with intense force on the minds of the populations, and that as true piety declined, and the patriarchal verities faded, these rose gradually into the place of more august truths, and furnished the traditional ingredients out of which idolatry was moulded.

Such a system once in motion would be sure to complicate itself by degrees, both with metaphysics and with naturalism, and by giving and taking from them would come to present constantly shifting combinations of outline. The stars, the moon, or, above all, the sun, would be sometimes imagined as the residence, sometimes as the personality, sometimes as the emblematic value, of the fancied god. To this he would be supposed to retire; from it he would then be fabled to have originally come, through it he would be regarded as habitually acting and manifesting himself by the agency of priests, saints, kings,

and heroes. Sometimes he would be identified
with it as a person, while at other times his
personality would be explained away into its
natural phenomena.

Here, in all these ideas, would be a basis upon
which different minds, schools, and ages might
rear systems either of materialism or idolatry,
planet-worship or rationalism, a religious basis
which would invite and co-operate with the
ambition of chiefs and of castes, lowering
as it would the whole tone of the population,
and preparing them, by servility of worship,
for imperiousness in law. For here, by these
means, the people would be deprived of the
practical influence of that old faith (ennobling,
however simply conceived) of the one divine
Father, Creator, Protector, and only supreme
Master of His creatures, the one great Name
to be reverenced ; the one fit Object of devout
contemplation, and of a friendly and family
worship ; the One alone capable of uniting all
ranks into a single religious brotherhood. The
parental relation thus struck out from its
position as the associating link between love
in heaven and love on earth would give place

to the idea of the father-king, who again would pass down into the despot. Traces of this transition of idea seem preserved in the Abimelech, or father-king of Scripture; the Padishah, or father-king of the Persians; the Atalik, "father" of the Khans of Bokahra, and other similar titles.*

The two real powers of the human sphere, the patriarch on earth and the Father in heaven, being thus removed from the foreground of society, and the want of them supplied by such reducing substitutes, we may be sure religion would soon cease, as we say, to speak its full language, and law soon cease to have its true force. But here, as in so many other cases, divine benevolence, through these intermediate evils, was working on towards ulterior good. The paternal conceptions of government, which had been realised in the earliest societies, though afterwards degraded in oriental despotism, had not been lost; they formed the basis for Mosaic legislation and for those ideas of individualism, of social right and responsibility which could hardly perhaps have

* Gesenius.

N

been developed without such a starting point,
and perhaps not even without such an intermediate stage.   They have, also, after the
passage through idolatries, possibly even by
some untraced movement in relation to them,
come to be the foundation on which have
rested the most affectionate and comprehensive
beliefs in divine superintendence and grace.
The individual can now return once more into
the family sphere. For the tribe is substituted
" the whole family of heaven and earth named
in Christ Jesus."   For the patriarch we have
the great Father of heaven, the object of
obedience, reverence,- and love, the fountain
of right and law.   The difficulties inherent in
earthly relationship come to be regarded as
temporary and less material. We can live in
patience through them and above them, while
here we are " seeking a country."   We are in
anticipation " citizens of heaven " of " the
household of the saints," and " heirs of
covenanted promise."

If the above observations contain any
approach to the correct idea of the progressions of society and religion, then it is evident

not only that civil life and spiritual life might
have something to gain from such a system as
that of Moses, but, further, that his legislation
supplied, with wonderful fitness, a want for
which there was no other provision, and that
the whole of Hebrew Law has a distinct place
and mission of the highest kind, and not in an
accidental, but essential, way in the development of these two great spheres.

Those who are aware of the slow growth
and inveterate tenacity of customs, who have
an adequate impression as to the lingering
parturition by which new ideas are produced,
and as to the gradual and complex arrangements by which alone they can become fixed
in the general mind, will not regard these progressions of religion and society as unlikely,
and will possibly see reason to think that,
among all the disintegrating forces of human
self-will in the past and the countless social
disorders which have so distressingly expressed
it, there has been at work an orderly hand
collecting and re-arranging the broken fragments of the first frame into a new edifice,
similar in design but far grander in proportion
and far more perfect in execution, than that

elementary method which went before; a temple which shall take the place of a tabernacle, a spiritual fulfilment which will work out into grand completions the outline of a type, and realise in a perfected humanity the truths foreshadowed in the commencements of patriarchal life.

The original and essentially true grade of the patriarch was subdivided as society advanced into those of father, king, and priest, moving in the three spheres of the home, the State, and the Church. The problems of history have been the phenomena of these areas;— efforts both to carry on the work of each and to harmonise their relations with one another. The solution of these problems advances as the great Author moves among His works, and Heaven itself supplies both a Father, a King, and a High-Priest. By principles, sanctions, and motive power it is incessantly gathering up and arranging the materials of an innumerable family, a chosen nation, a royal priesthood, in preparation for the splendid completion of the whole vast experiment of redeemed humanity at the appointed time—the "day of the Lord."

CHAPTER V.

We have described as the original idea of society a parent's tent, with children, and this transformed gradually into a patriarchal tent within a circle of tents of descendants. The known incidents of primitive life support this view ; our human origin, as God's children, seems to favour it, for a paternal commencement of society would surely lead to a paternal continuance of it.

We have supposed the patriarch's position one of great and increasing influence—great from his being the natural father, the dispenser of law, the recipient at times of divine communications, and the offerer generally in worship: increasing because the vast duration of patriarchal life would make this tribal chief a depository of far-reaching stores of tradition, and would place around him numerous generations of descendants. If one imagines for a moment a patriarch five hundred years old in communication with nearly twenty generations of his blood descendants, each more numerous than the preceding, it can well be understood that the latest of them would, when arriving at manhood, come to regard this venerable being, so reverenced, too, by their own immediate ancestors, as an object of almost superstitious awe, and worthy of worship.

We have further supposed that, as movements of society occurred, and the natural chief by relationship gradually gave place among adventurers to the chieftain of military command, there began to arise fresh communities which were the germs of the most ancient empires. These communities having the domestic incidents of the earlier patriarchal life (and domestic life is always something of a despotism tempered by the affections), and yet not having a real paternal tie between subject and chief to moderate them, would, by degrees, let in and even lead to great oppressions—oppressions further increased by the intermixture of conquered populations, the patriarchal thus degenerating into the tyranny.

The check and counterpoise to this danger, threatening human happiness, should have been

found in religion, but religion itself would
have been undergoing a concurrent decline,
since the august figures of the primæval tribe
leaders and founders of nations had, after their
death, grown to be objects of reverence in
religion. The cultus of ancestors had thus
interfered with the worship of the God of
ancestors. The two ideas had become inter-
mixed, and the simple beauty and truth of
man's relations to the unseen world were being
gradually lost.

A further cause of the decline of religion
would be that populations, conscious of the
fact of divine manifestations in the past, and
from spiritual decay, receiving them only in a
very modified degree, if at all, themselves,
would be eager listeners to every sound
seeming likely to be a voice of God speaking
in nature, and their minds unskilled to arrest
themselves at physical explanations of things
striking in the world around would pass up
easily to the moral sphere, and seem to see and
hear in such things desired communications
from the unseen world. The votary, who
already supposed himself to behold the home

of the translated patriarch in the distant star, would naturally enough listen to the thunder and catch the whisperings of the wind in the dark groves as expected voices from the spirit-land.

Religion, thus reduced, could hardly be any more an altogether protecting or moderating power among the rising discords of society. It was, indeed, itself on the quick decline to depravations more injurious than the worst things in civil life; and, instead of being the guide of man, was about to become his corrupter. The imagination of worshippers directed to natural objects soon came to picture some of them as special expressions, residences, or modes of communication with supernatural beings. Animals, trees, and a vast variety of things became mixed up in this fancy; and representations of them, or parts of their bulk set up in shrines, were considered as having like value and meaning. There is ever a relationship between the worshipper and the object of his worship. Cultus of the material soon brought in sensualism and cruelty into the rites, so that, according to the declaration of Scripture what they offered was in reality offered to evil spirits, what they got was an increasing vanity of the imagination and darkening of the heart. A proper band of acolytes soon swarmed up; fanatics, impostors, and evil men became the guardians and propagators of a system congenial to their progress. Thus, by a transition, gradual and easily followed, the beneficent influences of religion passed into heathen idolatry, which, as observed, far from being a palliative of social evils, was, on the contrary, itself the systematic perpetrator of the darkest enormities, and the direct corrupter of its votaries. The two lights of man were now eclipsed; religion was hidden in idolatry, social law in tyranny. The father in heaven and the father on earth were no longer heeded; and, while life here was made wretched, no real hope or consolation was brought from above.

Such were the two great growing evils, wound in together and complicated with the same cause, against which, if man was to be saved at all, even for this world, a persistent resistance must be made. This resistance and

remedy would evidently have to be sought in
the following directions—in a modified restoration of the patriarchal incidents and spirit, that
is, in the recovery of those social liberties,
allegiances, securities, and fidelities which
would naturally prevail in a family, whose
members should be organised under a father,
and influenced from above. The other part of
the remedy would be the restoration of the
original belief in the one God as the arch-
parent and protector, and reconstitution of
worship in accordance with this faith. It will
be found that these are exactly the ends which
the Mosaic system sets before itself, and that
the whole of its machinery, legislation, and
circumstance are incessantly pressing, with
successful strokes, towards these two results ;
so completely so that, if we bear in mind this
scope of the Scriptural plan, its working out
will arrange itself before us in clear and harmonious order.

One other point, however, remains to be
observed on. The two difficulties to be met—
viz., tyrannies in social life and superstitions
in religious life—that is, the non-paternal in

both the natural and spiritual spheres are, after all, only difficulties of a phenomenal sort. They do not go down to the very root of the matter, but they allow, and, indeed, presuppose something beyond themselves. That deeper difficulty is the fundamental one, the condition of the heart and will in man; and it is in the depravation of these that we are to look for the complete and final cause of his incessant tendency to break away from the true and happy in religion and in life. As a final and fundamental object, then, of the Mosaic revival we have to add, besides and beneath the two already-named works, this further one —a restoration and rebuilding of the inner life of humanity. Such, if the mission of Moses be really divine, must be its object and scope; and such we clearly see it is. It both professes as much, and also provides an adequate way for forwarding it. More than this, the way is one which dovetails in with a wider plan of world-order, commenced before in simpler beginnings, and continued long afterwards in deeper developments.

The whole problem, then, is as follows—to

restore religious and social life by restoring the heart of man. Neither part of the scheme is entirely to precede the other, but its three-fold elaboration is to advance simultaneously. Its methodical formula will be—" regeneration of the individual within a divinely framed order, and social life improved as a connected result." The society thus to be acted upon having been originally organised round the tent and altar of a father, who was also a chief, would move sometimes from a personal, sometimes from an institutional, basis. Its polity, imbued with affection, would now regard each as its sole object, and now again regard all as represented in the one. It would thus, when truly portrayed, exhibit to us a continuous interchange and transition between the personal and systematic ; the nation, at one time, appearing as a family, at another, receiving the most comprehensive laws as an individual, and then, again, spreading into the widest organisation of a commonwealth. Therefore the Hebrew is spoken of as follows: " Israel is my son," and yet " this nation is my people ;" and yet, again, " Ye shall be

gathered one by one, O ye children of Israel."
So, also, we have the blending of the thoughts
in such a term as " The kingdom of the house
of Israel," or as " He shall reign over the
house of Jacob for ever ;" phrases combining
the three ideas of individual, family and nation,
and applied, in Luke i., to the unending
kingdom of Jesus, in whom the social mystery
is to find completion ; so that He who has
stood in and fulfilled every attitude of relationship shall be both father and brother and
fellow-subject and king in the perfected Israel,
where all social and religious discords shall be
done away; where neither " the idolater, and
he that loveth and maketh a lie," nor the
unjust, cruel, and licentious shall be found;
where " there shall be no more curse, but the
throne of God and of the Lamb " shall be,
" and his servants shall serve him and shall
see his face, and reign for ever."

When we remember how incessantly the
relation of parent and offspring is reproduced
in life, the very universality of its application
and its productiveness of benefit express to us
God a parent, and God our parent. It is from

this point we may be sure that law would inevitably germinate; corruptions of law would be departures from this, restorations of law would be returns to it. Were one to require how to be released from the idol and the tyrant, the reply would be, " As the first and preliminary step you must find for us some eminent expression of fatherhood, and place him in emphatic relation to the divine Father. Thus alone shall we stand at the starting-point of religion and morals.

It is with such discovery that the Scripture revival commences. Its place is in the east, at the spot where population, descending the great river from the central mountains of Asia, had paused at the sea. From there action begins. A refluent movement takes back the father of Abraham to the garden plain, at the foot of the hills, and from this, again, separates Abraham himself by a second journey to another sea of the extreme west. The struggle of ancient affairs as going on in the Shemite tribes between the new life-methods and the old simplicity, between the " strange gods " of the town, and the one ancestral God of the tent circle, finds fitting expression among these emigrants. Lot, born at a quasi-religious centre, the town Ur, and a dweller at the town Haran, afterwards falls back in the new country into the town life under the King of Sodom. He is at once surrounded, and a sufferer by its corruptions. He ends, in his descendants, at the complete fall into its idolatries.

Abraham, the leader of the reformation, is kept upon the hills. The one "Lord, the God of heaven and God of earth," is there, his belief, worship, and policy. By this Name he swears the eldest servant of his house that his son shall not (like Lot's daughters) inter-marry with the idolaters around—a course apart under one father and one God, separate from false living and false beliefs, is the funda-mental plan passed on by him to his descend-ants. In accordance with this comes the vow from Jacob in youth that, if God wilt protect him, so that he prosper and return in peace to the loved father-tent of his oath, then Jehovah shall be his God, and the place God's house. From Jacob in manhood is divinely claimed this vow's fulfilment, "Arise, go up to Bethel (thy house of God), and dwell there, and make there (apart from contamination) an altar unto God, that appeared unto thee when thou fleddest from the face of Esau, thy brother." At once comes the revival, "Put away the strange gods that are among you," said Jacob to his household, "and be clean." "And they gave unto Jacob all the strange gods which were in their hand, and Jacob hid them under the oak which was by Shechem."

Following on such commencements there is a continuous growth of the revelation, while the tribe remains encamped in Canaan. There is a strengthening, also, of the patriarchal and tribal spirit in the presence of distinct and often hostile populations. The minute particularity, with which several hundred years afterwards the history was written down by Moses, is a proof, on the human side, how deeply the spirit of the earlier epoch had impressed itself on the character of the clans; a proof, on the divine side, how material to the whole system the incidents of that epoch were deemed by the wisdom of God. Its

value is evident to ourselves. The long-drawn
detail of patriarchal lives, which a careless
reader, over-impressed by later civilisations,
might suppose disproportionately expanded in
documents of an universal religion, has had,
in reality, invaluable effects. It has so stamped
the humanity of the patriarchs as to prevent
them ever becoming objects to superstition for
a cult. There they stand, deeply venerated
and most influential, at the threshold of the
national career, but still strictly historical,
distinctly human in their form, and too clearly
outlined in domestic feature to lend themselves
to be abused into ancestral gods. They thus
serve to retain the national mind constantly at
the historical level, with its origin clearly
before it, its founders merely ancestors of race,
and towering far above them all, totally
separate and beyond them, and yet intimately
related as benefactor, preserver, and covenant
promiser, the one unseen God of their fathers.
In an almost incidental way a very effectual
blow is thus dealt at polytheism, with its
mixings up of the human and divine. Whenever it gains a footing in the community it

P

can thenceforth be perceived to be a departure from the national attitude in religion, a wall of partition between the backsliding generation and the loved ancestors of the race.

This fulness of the patriarchal biography serves again a corresponding purpose in civil life. Its incidents illustrate and engage the sympathies in favour of the domestic tone to be taken in the Mosaic legislation, as to which, indeed, they are apologetic and a comment. The idea of family is placed by the narrative in so central a position that no future depravations of tyranny would avail to dislodge it. On the contrary, it has ever remained a constant witness and rallying point against them.

While the Scripture detail of patriarchal lives was thus throwing up a strong position against the dangers of idolatry on the one side, and of abuses of power, whether domestic or social, on the other, it should be added further that the third and most essential work of revelation was, at the same time, being concurrently advanced. The believer's course is, by means of these patriarchal incidents, set forth before the consciousness of God's people.

They see him making his ventures and struggles of faith, living and dying in trust, "not having received the promises." They see the full covenant ratified, its seals affixed, the typical Saviour persecuted by brethren, sold for silver, placed on the altar, lowered into the pit, sent on before into the distant land to be a preserver of life. At this point, which is essentially a crisis in the theory, we find occurring in the narrative that dramatic pause which indicates, in old writing, the close of a series and the approaching commencement of a new one. In this a further unfolding of the historical roll will show a fresh and progressive phase of the counsels of God.

Here we may observe that the concrete or historical, which is the Bible method, is, even on mere technical grounds, a fit basis of law. Legislation, though it is, in form, abstract, must, if it is to be applicable to affairs, arise naturally out of circumstances surrounding it. And, wherever such legislation has to commend itself to the approving judgment of a public, far removed from its scene in time and place, a recital of the circumstances is extremely appropriate and almost essential. This is so completely the case that, had the Scripture Law been less interwoven with narrative, its real bearings would hardly have been generally understood or appreciated.

The same sort of remark, indeed, might be extended further. In all revelations, if true, must be expected these qualities—that they will both follow man's history from the very first, and also, while retaining their own essential principles, that they will progressively change their aspects in accordance with man's stability and man's growth. For evidently revelation, if given at all, implies that man really requires it, and that God is really ready to meet his need ; and, since these needs of men and this disposition of God, if ever existing, will be continuous, the supply of revelation will continue likewise, nor will there be any time altogether without its influence. We shall have revelation attaching itself to history from the very first, and following it in epochs through its whole course.

A real revelation, therefore, will begin at man's beginning, will take on an historical form, will preserve its own ground-plan, and yet develope its teaching. It will follow us through our stages of civilisation, adapting itself to each, and yet will be all the time as wholly complete in itself as the manhood it accompanies and helps to mould. Totally different from this are such pretended revelations as that of the Koran. We come upon them suddenly, like the broken torse of a statue, to which pedestal, members, and head are wanting. They have no real consistency or further value than this, that they express the something wanting which they do not themselves supply. If the Bible truths rise at times into sudden prominence, they are like the abrupt coming forth of rocks, the result of real movements of a deeper power; and, if ever themselves isolated in appearance to the casual eye, they are yet, to the understanding mind, connected beneath the surface in consistent unity.

Such points of method may well be gone into for confirmation of faith in a day when Scripture is closely looked at. It may be part of God's dealing to hold in each generation

the balance of probability so poised that faith
alone may turn the scale. Such a course
would be both consistent with His general
proceedings and with our own make of mind.
If minute examination of Scripture detail
should ever raise any apparently unfavourable
presumption, no more fit counterpoise than
observations drawn from its general structure.
Tertullian noted at the first that heresy, which
explains away Scripture in general, is a worse
foe than that which aims at taking away its
particular parts. The same estimate will hold
good in answers to heresy. Proofs of the
Bible's systematic completeness will be more
widely conclusive than proofs addressed to its
detail; evident bond and cohesion in the
whole fabric more satisfying than completeness
observed in some particular part of it. He,
indeed, who rests content to attack a particular, unless it be one of a very central
character indeed, is confessing either his own
weakness or his adversaries' strength—for the
importance of the part is dependent on, and,
therefore, outweighed by, the whole. To be
unable to calculate this, or to avoid doing so,

are disqualifications for the office of deciding in so serious a matter.

We add, in general conclusion with regard to this period, that, had the tribe of Jacob remained in Canaan, their special character might probably have disappeared, and with it their fitness for their special mission. Already intercourse with the nations had begun. Canaan would have brought them in contact with errors of Egyptian origin without the restraints of Egyptian government. Mixed in with numbers greater than their own, they might have been led into the depraved manners and worship of the land. Removal to Goshen was once more refuge in an ark— for, while thus saved from the Canaanites, they were unharmed by Egypt. In a favourable isolation they could develope strength while retaining identity. Their work at that period being but a natural process—the growth of a tribe into a nation—a pause had accordingly to take place in the supernatural narrative to give them time to multiply up to the requisite size. Any detailed account of their history during that interval would have been as inappropriate as the apocryphal narratives of our Lord's childhood. A true biblical method requires they should be left in seclusion until the time of the next step would be at hand. The silence, therefore, with which Scripture passes over several hundred years at this point is an admirable indirect proof of the divine wisdom, guiding the great writer to a reserve which a mere national scribe would, under patriotic stimulus, hardly have observed.

CHAPTER VI.

WORLDLY changes often express movement by
the many; the crises of Scripture are usually
brought on by the one. It is, indeed, fit,
where the mainspring of action is a single
divine Person, that the agent, for the time
being, should thus appear as standing apart;
and that his mission, while not neglectful of
human qualifications, should be clearly seen
not to result from them; that there should be
in him a balanced composite power, springing
partly from natural tendency, long training,
and outer circumstance, but chiefly from a
divine message entrusted, and divine aids
given to deliver and get it attended to. A
minute examination of Scripture characters
might show them the exact products of such
joint causes. If so, this would be one of the
most scientific and complete answers to
mythical theories that could possibly be given.

Moses was clearly not one of those men
whom the times which require also mould

Q

and furnish with occasion. Such persons, while they are put forward, find a circle drawn around them beyond which they cannot pass. They move in front, but in step with their contemporaries. Without this they could neither lead nor be followed. Moses is not thus limited; not merely is he in harmony with the good of his age and in antagonism with its evils, his teachings rise into a distinctly higher sphere. So much so that the most civilised nations, even in the present day, believe him to declare the essential, absolute root of theology and morals; while his own countrymen, in their unparalleled vitality, though unable fully to follow him, still hold to him as the bond of their special life. To produce such results there is surely wanted not only a most happy combination of circumstance, but a further cause as well, so that the most difficult way of accounting for him must still be to suppose that Moses was not aided by heavenly revelation and support. For, even if it be imagined, for a moment, that parts of his action are hard to understand in connection with the divine; on the other hand, the whole of it becomes much harder to understand apart from the divine.

It was felt very early to be fit both that the Creator of the world should lay down laws for its government, and also should confer upon the words of His law a power to subdue men to conviction in all parts of the earth.* We have already partly shown reasons for believing God would thus legislate; we shall further go on to show this, and also that there is good ground for thinking the legislation of Moses is this divine work. For such a task, Moses is a wonderfully appropriate instrument. Following Abraham and Joseph, he appears, in his turn, a single figure on the scene; for, as the final completed salvation was to be by one, so, as observed, the typical and initial deliverance should be by one also. Each succeeding actor takes on the thread of the transaction; each, also, expresses a phase of the great future manifestation. The proportionate relations of a Bible character may be sometimes gathered from his entry. The infancy of Moses finds mention in Scripture, which is

* Origen contra Celsum I., xviii.

usually a sign of importance. Like that of
Jesus himself, it was surrounded with dangers.
Devoted to death, he is first found in an ark
at the sacred river of Egypt. The assailant
who is to overwhelm a superstition is thus, as
in our Lord's case, placed apparently helpless
in its very stronghold.

"The world," says one, "as if dimly fore-
seeing that Moses would destroy its work,
strove from the very beginning to annihilate
him; but, by his preservation in infancy, the
child, the predestined instrument of higher
designs, gives an earnest of his all-subduing
energy; and we are thus aroused to eager
attention respecting the further development
of such a life." * This passage from a leading
opponent of orthodoxy is observable. It
would, perhaps, be hardly fair to press it too
strictly, as it is rather rhetorical than argu-
mentative. Its method of dealing with the
subject is, however, an illustration of the
remark made above, that rationalism, in its
effort to remove wonders, frequently increases
them; and, by denying reasonable powers to

* Ewald Hist. Israel.

God, is obliged to heap inordinate distinctions on man: for here, in a single sentence, we have the world aggregated and acting in a corporate way; this entity is then supposed to foresee a world-enemy in a helpless infant, and to design and try systematically to destroy him. The child, again, is supposed predestined for a great work, and its preservation is looked on as a proof given by it already of an all-subduing force. Here are marvels, gratuitously offered, to which Scripture itself lays no claim; no such power is there arrogated to the infant Moses, or even to our Lord himself, though the apocryphal narratives of our Lord's childhood are, indeed, charged with them. It is with such accounts that rationalism competes, credulity and incredulity thus, once more, finding themselves in their perpetually renewed contact.

Already the "goodly" infant Moses must have been richly endowed, for he inherited in germ the ardent genius of Levi, the physical vigour of his parents, and that capacity of interest in the unseen protector of life which must have filled his mother when she put him down by the waters. Success, proportioned to his starting-point, might at once have been predicted for him. That starting-point became the most advantageous possible. Adopted by the daughter of Pharaoh, he had a complete training, during forty years, in the religion, politics, social science, and activity of the first country of the then world. Considering both the pupil, the teachers, and the school, we may regard Moses at the end of that period, as by nature, position, and acquirements, a man most fit to influence the events of his day. It is by no means surprising that tradition describes him as leading great expeditions for the Egyptians; it is very satisfactory as evidence that Scripture passes over such traditions in silence. The Jew, after many centuries, when the fame of the great legislator had become a national treasure and his precepts the object of fanatical allegiance, still aimed at enhancing his dignity and advancing his claims by rumours of his early Egyptian fame;* nor would a mere adventurer, with his way to make, have pro-

Josephus Ant. II.

bably been more reticent himself. The pen, however, guided from above, indulges us with no such recommendations. It draws no heroic features. It brings forward, without a touch in excess, a man called to a work of God. One quality it shows us in him which gave fresh value to the rest—Moses, in his Egyptian elevation, remained a Hebrew at heart. This it was which began his personal ruin and his long repute.

On his visit among his countrymen a circumstance occurred which separated him from Egyptian sympathy, and changed the early publicity of Moses for seclusion. At the hands of a human historian the crisis would, at this period, have arrived. The death of the Egyptian would have struck the spark, and the tribes, under their skilled and compromised leader, would have blazed into revolt. The Scripture narrative, on the contrary, dismisses Moses to a long retirement. True to its final moralities, it will not be implicated in the impatience of its agent. The future legislator records his own breach of his own future law and the penal sentence of his own transporta-

tion, and the movement—inconsistent with the
impatient proprieties of fiction, but in accordance with the long-suffering ways of Heaven—
waits for forty years.

A circumstance fixes the place of his banishment. He who is to become so great a helper
of the shepherds of the world assists the
shepherd daughters of the patriarch priest.
The same vigorous qualities now benefit which
before lost him, because this time they act
within allowed limits. Content to abide there,
Moses would find himself at the ancient
standing-point, in contact with the old patriarchal life and worship, and also with old
traditions of the Abraham stock; the dust of
former activity settling down would enable
him now also to discern, in his retirement,
what truths lay in his Egyptian past. Thus,
in the great cities of the world and in the
quiet dwellings of Reuel, " the friend of God,"
he would be made ready for his work as the
iron, through fire and water, is brought up to
its temper.

In such training the life had moved back
on its axis to the end of a second forty years,

and then it had become as apparently unimportant as when, in infancy, it lay in the ark. But, at this point, when a mere historian would hardly have taken it up, God finds it fitted for His work, and we discover the period of seclusion to have been the complement of activities in the past, and the preparation for them in the future. Regard its authorship as we may, such an arrangement shows a profound and true insight into the inner growth of life, and by its very opposition to ordinary methods lays claim to our consideration.

We have now, then, the man doubly disciplined, as the patriarchs Abraham, Jacob, and Joseph had also been. We have him living a patriarchal life among patriarchal traditions and sacrifices, and moving his flocks among sites held sacred. In him—so soon to be the leader—the nation itself almost seems once more moving in its free, ancient life, and expecting once more, by its prepared recipient, a manifestation of Heaven. He, too, is unconsciously ready for a revelation he has been fitted to receive and prepared to obey. What form, we ask, should that revelation be required

R

to take ?   What would reasonable expectation ask for as probable, and accept as fit?   Certainly there must be a revelation of some sort, for without it no movement could be brought on ; the man, in whom disinclination had become the crowning fitness, would not have stirred ; the Hebrews, who had been crying for direct help from their God, would not have stirred ; the Egyptians, a party very expectant of divine interventions, very much alive in testing them, very much interested in scrutinising this particular case, would not have stirred.

Unless it be pretended God is unable to reveal Himself, these expectations ask solicitously His intervention.   The long line of testimonies that He has answered seem really to need little corroboration.   They are themselves, indeed, proofs that He would be likely to do so.   We, in our time, have been gradually educated up to a point at which such things seem unlikely.   That is an excellent reason for their not occurring among us, but hardly a less good reason for a different course under different circumstances.   Every traveller expresses himself as he can; nor should we regard it as incredible that a reserved Englishman had, among Turcomans, explained his meaning by gestures, or addressed them through an interpreter of their own.

As to the detail of the revelation, we, at this point, say little, since its fitness will continuously appear. It would certainly have to arrange itself in accord with the traditions of the past, the emergency and agents of the present, and the progressive development and final scope of the future. This, though a wide requirement, will, we believe, be found fulfilled by the Bible in a most eminent way.

We may, however, here pause to make several observations with regard to the inner substance of the undertaking. Scripture, in producing a successful Moses, had a most difficult task, which a mere Jewish writing, not divine, could not have accomplished; for the legislative work of Moses had to be done in accordance with principles not then accepted, by methods not then fully approved, and in relation to a theory only developed by degrees in after ages. It had to be feasible at the

time, and yet consistent with after times.   It
had to be Hebrew on the surface, and Christian
within.   It had to connect the extremes of
divine policy and human capacity.   It had to
fit itself at once to an infant community in a
dark age, and to the eternal counsels of the
God of all light.   A Scripture to be in the
epoch of Moses a real link in the great coherent chain of advancing truth, would have to
do what no accidental arrangement could
possibly achieve ; and the success of Scripture
in the matter is itself a high proof it is from
God.

Suppose it suggested against us that Scripture—and especially such parts of it as the
Mosaic action—is but an accommodation of
more modern to more ancient ways of looking
at things ; an accommodation unconsciously
adopted on the part of the people, and in part
consciously by the writers dealing with facts
for the people's use, and throwing them for
the people into the older and acceptable forms.
That process, we reply, might produce a certain
smoothness of surface in the writing, but it
could never produce the internal harmonies

found in Scripture. It would not account for its essential ground-plan and organic development. It would still leave us this heavy difficulty to deal with, that the history should have been cast in a form, of which its early writers could not possibly have foreseen the future significance; and yet that a later set of actors, themselves neither free to mould their conduct, nor conscious of how much they were about, should so move in concert with what had gone before, that a relation should result, obvious to neither one nor the other at the time, and yet so minutely connected and harmoniously complete as to lead the large majority of us, who are at the right point of view, to feel that assuredly we are looking on no accidental combination or human arrangement, but that we are in the presence of a higher divine Power.

But let us look at the matter a little more closely. It is thus put by the respectful mythologist :—" The true and imperishable in Scripture," he says, "is not the event, but 'the spirit of the event,' and this, ' through countless variations in its reproductions, always

beams forth like a bright ray gaining greater
purity and freedom ' as the ' more evanescent
parts' drop away under the purifying influence
of time." This is meant to say, in graceful
and dignified form, we have not, in this Scripture, a statement of circumstance before us,
but a parable, founded on some circumstance
or other ; and this parable expresses from the
time, and for it, an inner truth of its life ;
something it felt, and passed through ; its mental
attitude then and continuously ; and parable
follows parable in a whole series, each always
basing itself on some outer circumstance, real
or imagined, but arranging it so as to express by
it its own same inner truth and idea essential
to its life ; and, though each generation has a
real history, and knows something of it, yet,
partly in its own hands, and more still in the
hands of its successors, this history disappears,
and assumes an heroic, unreal form ; that form,
however, expressing an inner, higher reality,
inshrined in the feeling and mental state of the
people.

Now, if we look at this a moment, we find
we have here a remarkable state of things, a

truth in an untruth; a perpetual evaporation of circumstance and notion deposited in its stead. We have in man an eternal want, arising and repeating its request; the mind incessantly looking out to find its answer, and, even in its emergency, seizing and making shift with the hard form of outer event, and for ever converting this from its actual state into a changed state, in which it can express an answer the mind wants to hear; and the mind, thus finding in echo a reply to its own speech, and in reflection of itself a personality with which to hold communion, and so, from time to time, throwing away the husk of old incident and taking up fresh, and again making belief, like a child-play, and still finding nothing outside to lay hold on, but moving still among shadows, echoes, and reflections of self. This is to portray a world reduced to strange shifts.

Surely it seems a roundabout sort of philosophy which, while it allows nature to be an universe, governed on the principle of real supplies in answer to real demands, yet introduces a humanity always demanding what is essential (since its universality proves the demand this), and never getting any real answer at all, but brought down to the expedient of a sort of perpetual chamber-idolatry, making a Maker for itself.

It is, indeed, only a subterfuge after all to tell us that, if Moses never did a miracle, or made a law, or even lived at all, the Bible account of him is still an essential verity. It would be no more so than if his picture, painted on a wall, had written under it "a prophet," and were insisted on as a substantial realisation, because expressing an idea present in the painter's mind. Revelation professes to be God answering; but, if it only turn out to be man questioning, what does it reveal?

The fact is, neither Moses, the man, nor his history, nor his system, can be got rid of. Modern probabilities against the narrative will not do it, for the basis of probability shifts. It is improbable that a man should be whipped like a school-boy, or dandled like an infant; but it is not improbable he was whipped when a school-boy, or dandled when an infant.

Neither can doubts be successfully brought against the historic personality of the Mosaic.

The theory of the mythus, its assumption of a personage as a hero of poetry, and its further transfer of the result to the historical attitude, are clearly marked by theorists on these matters.* But the Moses of the Bible does not lend himself to such transitions, nor does the Bible generally show traces of the process. For we have notably in it a series of primæval characters, such as Adam, Abel, Enoch, Noah, who would have been the very materials for mythus, and who would, by that process, have been amplified out into the proportions of Olympus or the Mahawanso, and who yet show in the Scripture no trace of either eastern or western mythus having touched them. On the contrary, they occupy their positions there with remarkable reserve, and are only unveiled at all at points of their necessary connexion with the essential framework of the system—a system, the real outline of which was only partly known even in the whole Hebrew time. There is not, then, in the early Scripture generally, nor is there in the person of Moses himself, this imagined tendency to the mythus. The man,

* Heyne's 'Apollodorus,' Part III.

as presented to us, is plainly historical and unheroic. Though grand in the highest sense, he is without the dramatic proprieties of grandeur with which imagination, and especially oriental imagination, always seeks to drape its favourites. Though he rises to heights, and achieves results to which patriotic fiction would hardly aspire, his career, at the same time, throws shadows such fiction would not consent to put in. The first failure in Egypt, the long banishment ensuing on it, the idolatry of Aaron, the leprosy of Miriam, the exclusion of the people, and, still more, of the prophet from the land, are not the acceptable form in which the mythic would come to life or survive.

Or, again, let the opposite alternative be put. Let the assertion be that some one of the times of Ezra pieced together ancient legends and documents, so arranging them as to get credit and authority for a system of law and government to be introduced among the exiles returned from the East, and that all this dignity and wonder was piled up to commend that system for acceptance by spicing it with ingredients palatable to the vanity of the nation.

In reply to this, consider the facts as they
stand. Moses is not claimed in Hebrew Scripture as exclusively national. He is described
as long a frequenter of the Egyptian court,
and learned in the policies and beliefs of the
land. He is again admitted to have long
dwelt among the shepherd chiefs of Midian,
and to have married, and had his children
born there. It is allowed in the Bible that
during a long life there had been only one
point at which he had come in contact with
his people, and that in this they had rejected
and ruined him. The mere comprehensive
vanity, which is a shadow of patriotism, would
here have been picturing in such a career a
tribute to the Egyptian system, or to desert
habits, rather than to the Israel which had
done so little for the great prophet. It was
at those two contrasted centres he had moved,
and there his powerful nature had assimilated
whatever was valuable and true, both in the
experiment and civilisation of the active Nile
valley, and in the long custom, the grand
primeval rites and traditions which lingered at
the Persian Gulf.

Moses was, by actuality, a compound of Egypt and Arabia, and it was only in his veins and in his sentiment that Goshen lived. As he stood among his flocks at the solitudes of Sinai, already awful in ancient report, the staff on which he leaned might have been looked at as the double emblem of an Egyptian ruler and a Midianitish chief; nor even if he himself, untaught by past experience, or unclaimed by present ties, had been likely to aspire to the work, could it have been at all likely that the Hebrews would have accepted in this double stranger, whom they had long ago, when much more powerful, indignantly rejected, a mover to rouse them to attempt so great an enterprise as the Exodus, or a leader to carry them through in it. And if the jealously exclusive tribalism of those returned from the Babylon captivity had, as is pretended, handled and recast these documents according to their own frame, we may be sure that those who then refused all assistance from their neighbours, though worshippers of the same God, who excommunicated their priests and chief men for contracting marriages with them, and who insisted on divorces as a condition of continued association, would never have drawn, or left without repainting, a Moses, leader out of another bondage, reformer and lawgiver, whom they were building on, with these uncongenial features about him of an experience altogether foreign, and a marriage and family outside of the tribes; but that when they did leave him so it was because they were not creating antiquities for themselves — a process most discordant with their tone—but because they felt themselves compelled, by facts well before them, to accept with veneration a claim, the credentials of which they knew were not patriotic, but divine.

Such a composite individuality as that of Moses, though foreign to Hebrew taste, is obviously valuable, and is found as a general characteristic in divine transactions, both in Scripture and in the world. Abraham, Jacob, Ezra, and Nehemiah, and many more, were personages of very diversified experience. Among communities, too, the intermingling of diverse elements is the most frequent condition of progressive change.

When the moment of his call had come the sign to Moses in the solitudes of Sinai was the wild thorn-bush of the desert, with a fire glowing in its midst, and yet unconsumed; emblem of the people cast down, but not destroyed; emblem of frail humanity safely pervaded by the Spirit; a picture of the present and promise of the future, and related in its form to the connected event in Gen. xv. 13. Moses, unlike Pharaoh, "sets his heart to the matter," and turns to see "this great sight." God, therefore, makes more known to him. He tells him he is at a holy spot and proclaims Himself the ancestral God; the Being of whom he has long been hearing and meditating. To him the affliction of Israel is known and their cry has penetrated, and He, in answer, has come down to take them to the good and large land, and Moses is to go to Pharaoh to bring them out.

His objections follow in so natural an order that they strike us as coming from the very mind of the living man. With the instinctive impulse of one knowing Egypt well, he is described as recoiling at once from the disproportionate idea of collision between a private person and the great Pharaoh. This is met by a grand reminder that he will not be alone, but that God will certainly be with him, and so effectually that, on the very spot where he is then standing, he and the people shall serve God. But this " I will" of the heavenly promise brings to the hesitating hearer the question, " Who, after all, is this Being who promises ? What his name and attributes?" This question must have existed in his own mind, for he feels it will be asked of him in the place where he is told to go. Thereupon the divine name is given. It is a claim to supremacy over all Pantheons, the expansion of patriarchal truth, and the realisation of the final fact which is concealed under the mythologies. God, who speaks, is the One self-existent, eternal " now," the " I Am ;" Jehovah (Ω ΩΝ), on whose life reposes the life of departed Abraham (Luke xx. 37), the God still of His removed saints. This is His world-wide witnessing ; this His name for ever. But next Moses objects, " they will not believe me ;" they will say " Jehovah hath not appeared unto thee." To meet this three signs are given to him to be worked in order. 1. The sign of power, pastoral and royal; the staff and serpent. 2. The sign of power in afflicting and healing; the leprosy caused and cured. 3. The sign of power by water and blood; a power over the heathen Gods. Still there is doubt. Inadequacy of position, insufficiency of information, suspicion of distrust are answered; the prophet is nearly at the end of his resources. He comes again at the fifth, as at the second point of the manifestation, to his personal unfitness.

He has not eloquence to persuade, and here as there he is assured God will be with him. And now having exhausted all excuse he plainly begs another may be sent. The anger of Jehovah is kindled, and the insufficiency of this first instrument brings in an added agency in Aaron. But the checks of God are ever advances; and here a fresh type is shadowed forth, and the foundation for a vast ministry prepared.

The refinements of this narration seem hardly from a human hand. No Jewish writer would have detailed an experience at once so spiritually exact and so derogatory to the fame of his great countryman.

Moses returned to his father-in-law, who knew not the undertaking, and then, with his wife and children, in obedience to a divine call, departed on the way to Egypt. Another incident here claims attention. He is going there an express agent to magnify the covenant, and to carry it out. The essential, invariable seal of that covenant was circumcision; " My covenant will I stablish in Isaac;" and "he that is born in thy house must needs be circumcised," and he that is not, "that soul shall be cut off from his people; he hath broken my covenant " (Gen. xvii. 12). And yet the son of this Moses whom he was taking with him was not circumcised. Whatever differences there may be in interpreting the transaction, several points remain clear. Jehovah met the missionary party on the road, and sought to inflict a death. The rite of circumcision was thereupon performed, and the death was averted.

These facts are not immaterial. By this transaction, placed in the very introduction of the mission, there is advertised to all the

T

information proper for a peculiar people, that
the equity of God is absolute. It is even a
warning, given on the forefront of Hebrew
history, that the Lord will expect special
exactitude of allegiance from those who are
brought specially close to Him, that He will
be honoured in those who draw nigh to Him.
Though the circumstances are so incidental in
form, they yet contain at starting a principle
sufficient to explain the whole Hebrew history.
They account to us for the severe judgment
which fell upon the sons of Aaron, which
swept, at intervals, over parts of the people,
which condemned the whole of them to the
wilderness, and which, at last, prevented both
the high priest and the prophet from entering
the land. They also · forewarn in figure concerning the fortunes of the Church. This first
passage of the ministry of death at the
beginning of the series has a remarkable relation to the similar one at the end of it ; for in
each there is danger, not only to those against,
but also to those described as on the side of
Jehovah ; and in each the danger is done away
by a special act, circumcision in one, the blood

of the passover in the other; and these two
rites, thus distinguished as life-preserving, stand
at each end of the Hebrew system as characteristic, and then pass on from that into the
Christian Church as the two special sacraments
of Grace, bearing close relation, baptism to
circumcision, and the Lord's Supper to the
Paschal rite, and themselves expressive of
redemption in its highest realisations.

The covenant was now in manifested activity,
and had begun to assume in shadow the outline of the Christian scheme. The people
who had cried in their misery had been heard
by God; and this, as He professed, for the
sake of one after His own heart. He had
remembered His promise, and provided them
a deliverer; had gifted him in type with
endowments of the gospel to overcome evil
and to heal disease and sin, and had already
arranged at the sacred spot, where He had
revealed and was soon to glorify His name, to
receive the national foreshadowing sacrifice of
His people. His ambassador, commissioned
and warned, was now to go down into the
field of a conflict supremely momentous to the

Hebrew race in its outer incidents, and also to the whole human race in its inner meanings.

As the representative of the future Saviour approaches, the representative of the future Church comes forth to meet him; and then, coalescing into one typical agency, the pair go on, first to the people, and then to Pharaoh. The monarch refuses to let Israel go, ignores Jehovah, speaks of his summons as " vain words," and weights the people more, lest through idleness they should be led away. The first movings of the divine work here as usually are disturbing to the oppressor, the oppressed, and the agent of rescue alike. Pharaoh fears disorders, the Hebrews destruction, and Moses failure. God again announces His name, Jehovah, the power of which, as expressing His sole and eternal existence, He will now begin to show forth; redeeming Israel, planting them in His land, and taking them to Him for a people. In their misery they give no heed, and Moses, disheartened, shrinks from the mission. The Lord now gives to him and Aaron a solemn commission for the Exodus. Their genealogies are recited, and, going in to Pharaoh, they do their first miracle.

CHAPTER VII.

WITHOUT here entering at length on the question of miracles already considered elsewhere,* we may yet observe in passing that, apart from them, no immediate outer manifestation of God to us is possible, such manifestation being itself a miracle. Neither without them could God manifest himself mediately through an agent; for, without the credential of miracles, men could not distinguish the ambassador from one acting by mere natural activity and boldness, and impelled either by policy, deceit, or madness. If we give up miracles, we must give up revelation; we cannot any longer keep Moses or Jesus on the scene without violence to consistency, and we then shall have to consider that the Author of the world is satisfied to govern us by law, rising altogether in the ordinary mind. But here a new difficulty would come in. By our effort to escape a prophet we should surround

* Lectures on Early Scripture, VII.

ourselves with a host of them, and the prerogatives we withdrew from God we should
be obliged to confer upon men. Such an
extreme imputation of almost divine power
will be found actually laid upon Moses, as on
others, by those very writers who would cancel
the supernatural element in the Bible account
of Him.

There is no course, we may be sure, so
economical of marvels as that which the Scripture has actually taken, and any attempt to
reduce the sum of them will only aggravate
the difficulty it is intended to remove. After
all, the miracle, in some form, is a necessity,
and the naturalistic substitutes for it show this,
since they are only miracles in disguise. If
the Scripture demands faith, rationalism makes
equally extensive claims. The writer who
endeavours to account for Moses in the mere
natural method asks us to picture his period as
one of " exceptional grandeur;" to regard the
man himself as of " surpassing greatness;" as
" an unparalleled hero, sustaining the grandeur
of two perfectly distinct, yet equally exalted
epochs;" " as a power, which produces the

mightiest and most lasting effects, and yet works in a mysterious privacy;" "hard to apprehend in itself; especially difficult for us, in our time, to penetrate." He is asserted to have given the first currency to truths which are still sustaining and protecting us, and in the hourly enjoyment of whose blessed fruits we still live.*

Why, when there is placed before us a personage like this, described to us as so excessively great, and as having produced such incalculable results, is not the very man himself a miracle? He transcends altogether the natural scale, and has become a problem quite as difficult as the Moses of the Scripture he is intended to supplant. Let but the power be allowed to God which the rationalist claims for himself—the power, that is, of putting on the scene an adequate agent, and the whole narrative runs smoothly enough—strangely, mysteriously, no doubt; but not more so than becomes the passage of a God in the crisis of a world.

The matter appears, then, to stand thus.

* Ewald's 'History of Israel.'

There is confessedly a stupendous fabric of consistent result to be accounted for. Three methods of explanation may be adopted. It may be denied that Moses ever existed at all, which, as Ewald truly says, is but an effort of despair. Again, it may be attempted to describe him as a mere natural hero, which, as we have just seen, really raises as great or greater difficulties than those it seeks to evade. Or, as a third alternative, we may simply accept the Bible account as it stands. And why should we leave it, when such feeble substitutes are offered in its stead?

Let it be assumed, then, there was a divine intervention at the time of Moses, and, we ask, who will deny that the results, in their dignity, in their immensity and lasting importance, have been worthy of such intervention? Who, again, will deny that the crisis was one which, if God can be possibly supposed to intervene, would be fit for His arrival? And who, we venture to add, will be unable to feel, on reflection, that the method of action is coherent and organised in itself, and harmonious both with what is described as preceding and following it; harmonious, that is, not merely in its outer structure but in its whole organisation and motive idea?

We must remember that it was not so much the Hebrews who made the law as the law which made the Hebrews. Their struggle for independence, their settlement in their land, their power of resistance and rebound, and their wonderful tenacity of national life, are all activities twined round the central spring of the law, for the purpose of receiving which they were selected and brought out. Their inner and more spiritual mission is equally connected with it. Out of the law gradually arises by growth the moral system, the prophetic and the gospel itself. Nor does the law, which has these connections and powers in the future, come itself abruptly into being. It has close organic relations with the antecedents of the tribes, with their sojourn in Egypt, and with the patriarchal past. On this side it goes back to the beginning, as on the other it goes forward to the end.

As regards the circumstances surrounding the law's promulgation the Mosaic cycle of

miracles is confessedly wonderful, but they
have a strong foundation of probability in
argument. The crisis required them. Suppose
Israel kept in Egypt there would have been
no social legislation; no religious revival.
There would have been no organisation of
Church or State, within which judges, prophets, kings, and statesmen could rise and
move. There would have been no Bible
influence on other nations, no Bible school of
morals, no cradle or Calvary of Jesus, or
stepping-stones for His Church. The divine
system, instead of unfolding itself in gradual
progression, would have been arrested. There
would have been a triumph of evil and of
man's enemy, and the much-needed promise
would have remained unfulfilled. In such a
great crisis we feel it likely great expedients
would be used, and we believe God does not
shrink from great expedients. The whole
plan of religion and our Saviour himself fully
show this. So, too, does all nature which is
not merely an inflexible order, but recurrent
periods of order portioned off and originating
in crises, so that the world's system is made up
of debris of storms.

Further, there was every prospect the good cause would fail. All human probability was against Israel coming out from Egypt. There was not the smallest ordinary chance in their favour. Withdraw the Bible account and no one can explain how they got away. That they were in Egypt is certain. The whole Law is tinged with convincing indirect proof of it. So is the narrative. Reject their own account of their deliverance because it contains theological miracle, and once again it will be necessary to give us historical miracle instead. In place of the wonder supported by long consistent analogies and relations of religion there will have to be put before us a wonder merely at variance with all experience of ordinary events. Why should we question the ancient account of the matter? If they had been inventing or re-casting their past they might easily have put together a more popular narrative. An inspired warrior like the judges, conquering against overwhelming forces, would have suited the times, the people, and the superficial symmetry of the case. If they abstain from this, give an account little flattering to themselves, and accredit God with all the success, is not that itself already in their favour? And if it appear that this account of theirs, though less likely on the surface, has yet under the surface many minute threads and attachments to the rest of Scripture, which could not have been observed or guessed at in their early time, but which greatly enhance its meanings, is not that still more in their favour?

Let us now go on to the texture of the narrative of the Exodus, and we shall find that as there is an observable gradation in the training and call of Moses, and in the delivery of his message to Israel, so there is, also, a gradation in the incidence of the visitations through which the people were rescued— the plagues in Egypt. Two powers are seen standing over against one another. In Pharaoh is collected the whole resisting force of that system, false in religion and despotic in rule, which is the organised strength of the secret world-tyranny, at once attractive and inimical to man. Moses is the apparently feeble instrument of attack on it; strong, however, in a divine truth,

a just principle, and an unseen heavenly
support.

And here we may observe that the whole
series of events is to the Christian an expression, extraordinarily vivid, of the fundamental
contest, still believed by us to be waging
among men, lying at the roots of life and
essentially affecting our prosperity; a contest
engaging, as we also believe, the interests and
energies of the whole invisible world. Scripture we look on as both the record of the war
and a great engine for carrying it out. The
characters and events recorded there are, as it
seems to us, incessantly reflecting in visible
colours the mysteries of the inner conflict.
May it not be possible that a large part, or
even the whole, of what is put down in Scripture has also further relations and resemblance,
not only to subsequent events here but also to
transactions beyond the present scene. Sometimes there are hints scattered, and hardly
discernible, which seem to point to this; at
other times when a crisis of the narrative is at
hand these suggestions seem to group themselves together, as if to express distinctly the

terms of the hidden transaction. Thus we
have Elijah set in contrast with Ahab, Daniel
with Nebuchadnezzar, Mordecai with Haman,
and the like. Still more have we Moses and
Pharaoh, David and Saul, picturing to us
beforehand the great mystery of time and
beyond time of Jesus conflicting with Satan.

Without attempting to define or systematise
this we may believe it to exist. There is
every antecedent probability that it would
exist, and there are most suggestive traces of
it throughout the Bible. If so, a Pharaoh
who has such meanings, a Moses who has such
a mission, rise at once in our minds to the
most vast importance. They become the
representative advocates and champions for
the widest interests, and by their means the
conflict of immense forces is being brought to
an issue. This the narrative partly professes,
but partly withholds. It is only when the
divine is actually present on the scene in the
person of our Lord, that a personal opponent
from the spirit world is clearly defined in the
field. But if we believe Scripture thus expressive it should not in the slightest degree

surprise us that at such all-important moments as the giving of the law, and of the gospel, we find attendant series of most pregnant wonders, serving as credentials for the systems they accompany; typically expressive of their course; but also, may be, projecting their meanings beyond us into an untraced sphere, and there, too, addressing combatants and spectators we know not of.

To a person who adopts this not unreasonable view it would be futile to object that experience of common history does not show events like the Exodus, for to him the Exodus has risen to proportions far in advance of mere national affairs, and therefore permits, and even requires, unusual phenomena to give expression to its meanings, and to be adequate to its importance.

But to return: the miraculous visitations of the plagues have, we said, an observable order pervading them. They arrange themselves into three consecutive groups of threes. In each triad a similar preparation is made. The first plague is preceded by an early and impressive warning; the second by a warning less marked and emphatic; the third occurs suddenly, without warning at all. The scale of the infliction, like that which Satan had himself chosen for Job, is also an ascending one, through property to person. The last sudden visitation in each triad is a pressure on the bodily life.

This increasing severity of treatment is a renewed preparatory warning for the . final crisis of death. It is also in correspondence with the way in which chastisement has been received. In the first plague of each triad Pharaoh makes concession, but after relief relapses and hardens his heart. In the last plague of the later triads it is God who hardens him.* At the end of the first triad even the magicians witness to the genuineness of the Mosaic wonder. At the end of the second triad Pharaoh is found resisting the magicians, who apparently counsel surrender. Each series thus culminates in an inner crisis of resistance. The policy of God is proclaimed and enlarged at the beginning of each triad. It is that by the wonders now working it may

* See Appendix.

be known that He is first the self-existent God, secondly the self-existent God in the midst of all the earth, and thirdly that for this very cause Pharaoh has been allowed to rise, that in him Jehovah's power may be declared through all the earth. These declarations, throwing a momentary flash of far wider suggestion, advance a stage in each triad.

There may also be noted a gradual rise in the demands on behalf of Israel, proportioned and related to the resistance met with, and to the gradual admissions and concessions made and withdrawn by the king. Beneath these seeming surrenders lies the final frame of Pharaoh. Neither the prophet, nor the divine Lord, nor the Egyptians, nor his court and magicians can affect the nether millstone of his inner life, and his last word to Moses— "Depart, see my face no more, for in the day that thou seest my face thou shalt die"— strikes the fatal chord, moving on the action to the last affliction. The tenth plague, completing the circle, returns back upon Egypt, though in a much mitigated form, the policy of death they had formerly planned against the infants of Israel,* and which began the movement by causing the oppressed to cry to the Lord.

It is well known, and has been carefully pointed out by recent writers, that the triad plagues are to a certain extent aggravations of natural phenomena, some of them still occasional and others still almost periodical in Egypt; a circumstance which enhances their historical and moral weight. Thus, it seems, the change of colour in the Nile water still happens annually after the end of June, when it becomes a dark red, though in this state it does not usually kill the fish or become undrinkable. The visitation of frogs still follows some time after the change of the waters, and creates occasionally great inconvenience. Travellers also describe the vermin at present as extremely distressing. Thus Sir S. Baker mentions a sort of tick not larger than a grain of sand, but which, when filled with blood, increase to the size of a small nut. The plague of flies is calculated as inflicted at about the end of October, a time at which the dog-fly is

* Exodus, iv. 22, 23.

now very troublesome. These flies come in immense swarms, and their painful bite causes local inflammation. In Egypt the cattle are in the fields from December to the end of April, and the disease would have come on them about the former period, at the time of their removal from the stall, when change of habit and diet would render them particularly susceptible. In recent years the murrain has several times fallen on Egypt, and so greatly ravaged the herds as almost to destroy them. Again, cutaneous eruptions of extreme severity, and accompanied with the symptoms described in Exodus, are still very prevalent in the valley of the Nile. Flights of locusts, too, still at times pass over and devastate it, and the south-west wind in spring brings immense clouds of fine sand from the desert, darkening the air far more than our worst winter fogs, obliging the people to take refuge in their inmost apartments, and occasioning that oppression to the lungs which leads us to class this plague at the Exodus as a bodily infliction.

A most important connection has also been

partially traced between the plagues and the
Egyptian religion, going to show that each
succeeding infliction was not only a fresh blow
on their affairs, but also a fresh confutation of
their theology, and that the whole was a progressive exposure of the impotence and nullity
of their nature-gods, imagined by them to
preside in those spheres of life in which
Jehovah now showed Himself supreme. Thus
the Nile was sacred and an object of cult; the
frog was connected with their most ancient
nature-worship; symbolically the earth smitten
in the third plague was regarded as the
father of the Gods; their insects and cattle
had symbolical meanings; and to them
Pharaoh was representive of man and God,
on whose forehead the serpent expressed
the royal and divine, and who was the
protége of Ra, the sun-god, chief object of
their worship.

It is not unlikely that the advancing knowledge of Egyptian antiquities may cause this
meaning of the plagues to be drawn out with
convincing accuracy, and show how valuable
and perhaps essential an introduction they

must have been to commend the legislation of
Sinai to the Hebrews, and by degrees to the
world, and to secure obedience to that rule so
difficult it seems to ignorant and learned alike,
that one personal Jehovah governs in heaven
and earth, and that he is to be worshipped
without similitudes in spirit and in truth.
How great an impression that way the whole
transaction had made may be inferred from
the song of Moses at the moment of their
escape, "Who is like unto thee, O Lord
among the Gods? Who is like thee, glorious
in holiness, fearful in praises, doing wonders?"

In estimating the documents we should constantly remember that the time of Moses is a
crisis in the Bible. The transition from the
patriarchal to the national, it is next in importance to the epoch of our Lord, which
is the transition from the national to the
universal. Like the giving of the gospel,
therefore, the giving of the law has to be
attended by the credential and exposition of
miracles, and first among these are naturally
the miracles of release, freedom of the will
going before obedience to the rule. Pharaoh

being the apt representative of the hostile world-power, his conflict with Jehovah is found leading to destruction. Moses being the representative of heaven, his mission, therefore, leads on salvation. We are thus brought to the last plague and the first sacrifice; the death of the first-born, and the offering of the paschal lamb. The two occur in relation, judgment and mercy here, as elsewhere, being linked together.

The boundary of Goshen had been a barrier against other plagues, but at the coming forth of the last death-causing attribute or agent, it seems a special protection was needed by the Hebrews. And this, on reflection, we shall feel was to be expected; for death, the consequence of sin, holds a judgment against all men, and when once moving can only, in the Scripture theory, be stopped and done away by one remedy. In the wonderfully complete plan, then, that remedy is now to be brought forward in representation that the typical history may work on towards its final proportions. A lamb is appointed and is set apart four days before the great judgment. Here, in connection with previous numbers,* the four-fold interval of time may possibly have reference to the deliberate patience of God.

There are senses in which the passover may be looked on as the chief of sacrifices and key of the system. It is first in time ; it is critical in emergency ; it is efficient not for ceremonial remote, or unseen consequences, but it saves from immediate bodily destruction ; it is offered without priests and without an altar; each head of a family himself applies it in his own home, and for all his house—for all, we say, since, though a terrible, the death of the first-born is still a restrained and representative expression of completer judgment; the first-born stand vicariously, and are representatives of the saved something as the lambs are of the Saviour. And, further, the first-born being saved, when due to death, by a substitution Jehovah has allowed, are for ever after regarded not as independent but as belonging to Him, and they always have to admit this by being redeemed for a price. Thus the whole trans-action of salvation is at the very beginning

* Genesis, xv. 16.

expressed as vicarious; the lamb is clearly shown as the substitute for the sinner who belonged before to death, and who, on being saved, belongs to the Lord—"The people whom Thou hast purchased." If the lamb and the Lord be identified as one and the same, the plan of the Gospel is here before us. The blood upon the top and upon the two sides of the door might almost in this connection seem the mark a Saviour already fixed there, with outstretched arms barring the passage against death. When the angel charged with the ministry arrives, he sees that judgment is already satisfied; death already there; he reverences the mystery and passes.

No Israelite had neglected the rite, for at that particular moment Israel was to express as against the enemy the completeness of salvation through the blood of the lamb. But had a single house omitted it, there we should have expected to find ensuing those consequences which, in Leviticus, befell the one who broke the Sabbath.

The lamb having represented and, indeed, effected preservation out of death was further to mean building up in the unity of life. It now had to stand for the strengthening and refreshing of the soul by the body and blood of Christ. The Israelites, with loins girded for their journey, in the strength of that meat, go forth like Elijah towards the mount of the Lord. It is a meal of pilgrims and strangers who seek a country, and it is eaten with bitter herbs by those who, through much tribulation, are to advance towards the kingdom of God. Again, it is a meal of union for those who being many are thus made one bread and one body.

It is once more a meal of separation also, since the old leaven is purged out, and the feast is kept with the unleavened bread of sincere service to a true God. Thus the patriarchal epoch draws to a close in full consistency with the truths which have pervaded its course, and which in a higher form are yet to follow it, and, as at the beginning when the whole nation was shut in the loins of Isaac, the son was placed on the altar by the father, instead of animals usual at the time, so here, at the end, as the crowning idea of the preliminary system, the animal again takes

the sacrificial place and stands alone, instead
of the many sons of Israel. No intermediate
machinery of ritual, altar or priesthood arrest
the thought, but we are carried straight on to
the atoning blood itself, pleaded by each
father in his own home, and effectual there to
save and to sustain. A more beautiful epitaph
on the dynasty of the patriarchs cannot be
imagined, speaking like other epitaphs of that
which has departed, and which is to be found
again.

The Hebrews, thus sanctified, now begin
their march. The glory of the Lord is risen
upon them, and they go forth as His host in
orderly array and in a festal attire, which is
not, as sometimes thought, the unduly gained
property of their oppressors, but a voluntary
ransom from the Egyptians to be freed from
the danger of their presence. They pass on,
attended by a multitude who cling around
them—a first wave-sheaf of the earlier harvest
of the Gentiles, already dimly perceiving the
truth of Abimelech ; "We saw certainly that
the Lord was with thee."*

* Genesis, xxvi. 28.

A great layman, to whom physical science is indebted, wrote his confession of religious faith. He believed that in the person of the Mediator, the Lamb of God slain before all worlds, the true ladder was fixed, whereby God might descend to His creatures, and His creatures might ascend to God; and that transactions with respect to the Mediator make the great mystery and perfect centre of all God's ways with His creatures. That "among the generations of men He elected a small flock (*i.e.*, the Hebrews), in whom, by the participation of Himself, He purposed to express all the riches of His glory—all the ministration of angels, damnation of devils and reprobates, universal government of all creatures, and dispensation of all times; having no other end, but as the ways and ambages of God, to be further glorified in His saints, who are one with their head the Mediator, who is one with God."*

Thus, the man who led on a revolution in science saw in religion a system already complete. He believed that the law of God and

* Bacon.

the word of Ilis promise endure the same for
ever, and were, from this time of Moses,
expressed partly in the written code, partly by
a double series of figures; the one, the rites
and ceremonies of the law; the other, the
continual history of the old world and the
Church of the Jews; which, though it is
literally true, yet is also "pregnant of a
perpetual allegory and shadow of the work of
redemption to follow."

In which opinion this great mover of thought
was content to remain quietly fixed, together
with the whole of the prophets and teachers of
the old and new Scriptures, and with the
general consent of the whole ancient and
modern Church, as far back as record goes;
all of whom have accepted this fulness of
meaning in the purpose and plan of the Bible,
and seen in every part of it, as he saw "the
one Jesus, the Lord, become in the flesh a sacrificer and sacrifice; a satisfaction and price to
the justice of God; a meriter of glory and the
kingdom; a pattern of all righteousness; a
preacher of the word which himself was; a
finisher of the ceremony; a corner-stone to

remove the separation; an intercessor for the Church; a Lord of nature in his miracles; a conqueror of death and the power of darkness in his resurrection; fulfilling the whole counsel of God; performing all his sacred offices and anointing on earth; accomplishing the whole work of redemption and restitution of man to a state superior to the angels; and reconciling and establishing all things according to the eternal will of the Father."

Or, to use for expression that eloquent form ascribed to Irenæus, "in all Christ was all; Patriarch among the patriarchs; Law in the law; the Priest among priests; among kings Prime Leader; the Prophet among the prophets; the Angel among angels; the Man among men; Son in the Father; God in God; King to all eternity. He was sold with Joseph; He guided Abraham; was bound along with Isaac; and wandered with Jacob; with Moses he was leader and respecting the people Legislator."

Whoever may hesitate to join himself in consent to this testimony and reasonable plan, will have three things to reconcile; first, that in so feeble a people as the Jews such a design should have sprung up of joining the world under one religion; secondly, that this design of theirs should, through many generations and ages, have been consistently pursued and expressed harmoniously by so many nearly unconscious instruments; and thirdly, that the project should have come to the measure of success we see in our day. Beforehand it might have seemed wonderful to persons who had little considered the subject that such things should be truly from God, but now, afterwards, when they have gone so far, it would be a great deal more wonderful that they should be mere false inventions of men.

As the people are leaving Egypt a candid observation of the course of the narrative will show that thus far the purposes of Scripture have been completely answered. The one self-existent God has been revealed, and the common pantheon brought into discredit and disgrace. A people has been formed and has set out to preserve and spread the new manifestation. Their very first design is to establish a worship to represent it. No sooner are they free than this is proclaimed,—"The Lord is my strength and song, and he is become my salvation; he is my God and I will prepare him an habitation." A permanent outer expression of religion was a popular sentiment and need. But a dwelling for God was a plan which brought risks as well as opportunities. It has been the admirable wisdom of the Hebrew system so to build the ritual as at once to guard and advance the truths entrusted to it.

The same is the case on the social side—while the new vigour is added the old deposit is retained unimpaired. The unity of the system is so cared for that, though much is gained, nothing is lost. Though Jehovah is my God "still he is my fathers' God, and I will exalt him." Again, the defeat of Pharaoh is a moral shock to tyranny. Internal liberties of nations have begun to live, and are about to be organised under the law of Sinai. In the meantime the very first provision after the passover expresses the spirit which underlies the movement. It is for the admission of slaves to the privilege of the covenant religion*—a religion already stamped indelibly with family features by the rights of that first sacrifice.

Thus we have man's relations both for the world and for heaven advanced; sacrifice already arranged in periodic recurrence; patriarchal incidents grouping themselves in counterpoise to the hierarchical in the coming law; the attributes of the Divine revealed and partially embraced; the decline of a false faith commenced and approaches laid for a pure and true system; a breaking away begun from Egyptian chains—mental, spiritual, and social; and so a preparation of the people for the mission of their twofold obedience to earthly and heavenly duties; in other words, the ground is laid for the two tables of the law and for the ritual of worship, and this "kingdom of priests," fresh from its first experience of the values of the blood of the lamb, goes forth from bondage harnessed (or in battle array), the Lord going before them with signals of smoke and fire like the generals of ancient time.

* Exodus, xii. 44.

They have, too, in their midst a singular and significant relic—the mummy of the long-dead Joseph. They thus fulfil the oath he took of their fathers, and the two great types, Joseph and Moses, the bringer in and the bringer out, are thus, also, in actual contact of fact as well as idea, and as they carry the long-dead man down into "the depths of the sea," which "the Lord hath made a way for his ransomed to pass through," the whole transaction projects a most vivid outline of an all-important truth of later theology—the passage through the grave under the anti-typical leader, to a safe resting-place, where remote generations shall lie together; where there shall be no more tyranny of Satan; where they "shall not see the Egyptians again any more for ever" (Exodus xiv. 13); where "the tabernacle of God shall be with men, and He will dwell with them and they shall be His people" (Rev. xxi. 3), and where they shall "sing the song of Moses and of the Lamb."

CHAPTER VIII.

WHILE the history of the Hebrews, viewed from one point, advances in a continuous outer order, it yet appears, when regarded from another point, to express varied relations of the same one spiritual enterprise. Israel in Egypt explains the process of conflict between the Church and Satan, in which the divine Leader is seen treading the wine-press alone ; vindicating His sole supremacy, and getting Himself glory over the world-power, by the release of a people saved from death either through His own or the enemy's wrath.

Israel in Canaan no longer describes the great primary movers and very springs of action, but dwells on the immediate agencies, and paints the struggling Church in conflict with the organisations of time.

Israel in the wilderness is to put before us the intimate dealings between God Himself and His Church. The Scripture here shows us the Church led, fed, championed, covenanted,

ruled, taught, officered, and organised in all
things. It further shows us the conduct of the
Church; its joys, fears, complaints, promises,
backslidings, repentances, rebellions, movements towards and away from its goal; and
then how God, in and by all transactions of
forbearance, judgment, and remission, advances
His purpose in ever-growing ripeness of fulfilment.

The last echo of the holy song had hardly
died away when the first discord of the
Church's weakness striking on the prophet's
ear showed at once that the time for fully
accordant harmonies was yet far distant.
Moses, it now appeared, would have to be the
motive agent on the human side as well as on
the divine. Representative of Christ, his faith,
supplementing humanity, "against hope could
believe in hope," like Abraham. Like him,
he "staggered not at the promises of God;
being fully persuaded that what He had promised He was also able to perform." With the
people it was not so. "What shall we drink?"
was their question at Marah; for they saw
risk but no relief, though the pillar of cloud

was there before their eyes, and the wonders
of Egypt so fresh in their memory. Their
hearts did not rest on the Lord whom their
lips had sung as triumphing gloriously, and
because a well opposed them they forgot a
sea had just surrendered.

The work of intercession now proceeds in
the new field. "Moses cried unto the Lord,"
and "the Lord showed him a tree, which when
he had cast into the waters, the waters were
made sweet." The ancients, who saw Christ
in all, believed they here saw a type of the
cross. If it was so, the type was significant,
for here, at the very outset, the performance of
duty was made man's work, while the process
of cleansing was shown as Christ's work: whatever might be the future elaborations, it was
upon this, interpretation at once based its rule.
Not only at the time but in long subsequent
ages this was insisted on ; "I spake not unto
your fathers, nor commanded them, in the day
that I brought them out of the land of Egypt,
concerning burnt offerings or sacrifices ; but
this thing commanded I them, saying, Obey
my voice, and I will be your God and ye shall
be my people " (Jer. vii. 22).

The people had been forced to serve Egypt to their harm. God having purchased them, they were now bound to serve Him for their good. Pharaoh had been ruined, as Origen fully shows,* because he resisted warnings, providences, and his own convictions. The same idea of probation now begins to rise in the narrative for Israel. Already at Marah God gives a statute and an ordinance. A suggestion of uncertainty comes into the prospect. Blessing will depend on a faith which shall listen and obey. It is on such conditions they will escape the plagues of the Egyptians.

The water had, by the wood, been healed for them, and having been taught that it is Jehovah that healeth His people, they now, from the one bitter source, journey on to the wells and palm-trees of Elim (twelve and seventy—the numbers of both the old and new Church), and encamp there by the waters in peace.

The wilderness of Sin next advances the journey and probation. There is now a want

* Origen, De Principiis, iii. 1.

of bread.   This time it is not a multitude but
the organised people who murmur.   Their
complaint extends against Aaron as well as
against Moses.   Although the promise that
they should escape the plagues of Egypt, if
faithful, is fresh, and their late deliverance
only one march behind, they now openly
declare death in Egypt with the first-born
better than death in the desert.   The Lord's
presence is not in their consciousness; their
faith does not calculate on His help; their
disobedience repines at His service; they see
not salvation but destruction before them.
Aaron, therefore, has to summon them before
the Lord, and now they all behold His glory
appearing in the cloud towards the wilderness,
as if in front of them on their way.   Manna is
rained from the sky for them; and this food is
thenceforth given from day to day for many
years—the means to wean to spirituality their
carnal preferences, and to make them know
the truth, repromulgated by Him " who for
our sakes did fast forty days and forty nights,"
viz., " that man doth not live by bread only,
but by every word that proceedeth out of the

mouth of the Lord doth man live" (Deut. viii. 3, and Matth. iv. 4).

The victories of the Lord are never barren. With the six days for the bread of the body is given the one day for the word to the soul. The preparations for Sinai are in all this being rapidly brought on. Already (ver. 6) the truth of the second commandment is established. The declaration of the first commandment is anticipated (ver. 12), and the fourth commandment is set in action. The beneficent institution of the Sabbath, so essential and yet immediately found so difficult, is from that time perpetually being expressed and enforced by the withholding of manna on the seventh day.

The narrative now passes without detail several stages, thus showing truths and not circumstances to be its purpose, and then it pauses at the next place of trial and teaching, Rephidim ("supports"). Here there is no water. They demand it of Moses in anger, asking why he has brought them out of Egypt to kill them, their children and cattle with thirst. "We should not complain," says Bishop Hall, "if it were not good for us to want." How much they had to learn is shown by this, that it is still Moses and not the Lord they treat with. "If they had gone to God · without Moses I should have praised their faith," continues the same writer, "but now they go to Moses without God I hate their stubborn faithlessness." We disapprove, and yet Israel is the picture of ourselves (τύποι ἡμῶν) as the wilderness is of the world's pilgrimage and the dealings there are of God's present providence and grace.

The Israelites were no strangers to suffering; they had groaned under it in Egypt. They had cried there to God for help and He had answered. They had seen His enemies severely afflicted, but now they seem to ask why are His own people thus suffering. There was the cloud before them, but what availed it to be led if they could not live. Manna secured daily bread, but water was an equal need. Moses, the mediator, is there, but can the Lord Himself really be among them?

The Lord answers thus. Moses is ordered to go on before, accompanied by the heads of the people and to take his rod—"The rod wherewith thou smotest the river." As though he would say, He who in that case could stop the supply to deliver them would now, they might be sure, bestow it to preserve them. The appointed witnesses advance, and the presence of the Lord is seen there on the rock in Horeb. Moses smites the rock once, and the waters flow forth. This water it has been sometimes considered from that time followed Israel, either constantly or generally, as a river of supply, according to 1 Cor. x. 4. Thus in anticipation of Isaiah (xxxiii. 16), itself anticipative of greater blessings, "bread was given them and their waters were sure."

They were about to tarry "on high among the munitions of rocks ;" to "see with their eyes the king in his glory;" to have "the Lord for their judge; the Lord for their lawgiver; the Lord for their king." But first there must be a conflict with an outer enemy.

In Pharaoh, as we believe, was summed up and expressed the organised hostility of the spiritual foe of mankind to the Church of God. The passage of the Red Sea, and the final destruction of that power in those depths which were a way to life for the saved, who

were "to see the Egyptians no more for ever,"
removes this method of expression from the
field of the narrative; but as even the inter-
relations of God and the Church, which appear
the chief idea of the desert stations, are not free
from the external intrusion of this adverse spirit-
power, it was fit there should be found another
instrument of expression for its hostility. When
the thought had been mankind prostrate under
the tyranny of the prince of this world, and
many successive blows struck in history to
loosen his hold, and his final defeat by the
blood of the lamb, and his end in utter
destruction, then a great Egyptian king was an
adequate representative; but in the wilderness
this would no longer have been appropriate.
Jehovah is no longer, as it were, outside
seeking to release and take away his people.
He is now the victor present by a visible
manifestation as the leader of a settled Church.
That Church is the germ of an eternal
organisation which will itself be mystically
incorporated with the Divine. By the side of
these transcendent powers the Satanic chief
can no longer be properly represented as a

monarch on a throne. The state of things
requires malignity to be shown under a different aspect ; still watchful, pitiless, crafty,
and relentlessly cruel, yet with but the hostility
of the wild beast on the outside of the fold,
"seeking whom he may devour;" prowling
round; springing on at unguarded moments;
driven off; returning again, and only to be
escaped from by being destroyed.

The former series of events had represented
God rescuing His captives ; but this series is
to represent God reigning in His Church. The
enemy who was great in his own house of
bondage cannot now be great in the free
mount of the Lord. It is he this time who is
in another's territory. A type under these
circumstances, exactly appropriate for him, is
found in Amalek, who now " came and fought
with Israel ;" " smiting the hindmost of them ;
even all that were feeble behind them (and
had fallen into the rear), when Israel was
faint and weary" (Deut. xxv. 18). Just as
afterwards Amalek came up into Canaan in
company with the children of the East, "and
destroyed the increase of the earth and left no

sustenance for Israel; and they entered into
the land to destroy it" (Judges vi. 4). Just
as they also in David's time invaded the south,
burned Ziklag with fire, in the absence of its
male defenders, and took away the whole of
their wives, sons, and daughters, and went
their way; and when tracked by means of one
of their own slaves, who had been cruelly
abandoned by them in sickness, were surprised
in a brutal orgy of rejoicing at their great
spoil (1 Sam. xxx.).

We have this savage power now in the
wilderness treacherously hanging on the rear
of Israel, and we have Moses giving an order
to a new character, Joshua, at this time most
fitly introduced, commanding him to choose
out men and fight with the enemy. A double
type here connects the outer history with its
inner values. Joshua in the field below, whose
name means Jesus, is representative of the
Saviour as the warrior Chief of the Church
"going forth conquering and to conquer;"
Moses above in the mount, representing the
Saviour in heavenly places, is at the same time
carrying on that sustained intercession which

secures to his militant people their triumph in
the Lord. The raised and falling hands express
the necessity of this continuous intercession as
a condition of conquest, while the attendant
ministrations of Aaron and Hur admonish us of
the weakness of the typical agency in itself,
and suggest the twofold ancillary machinery of
civil rule and religious rite, by which the
Lord's battle is carried on in the world. The
altar of Jehovah-nissi is expressive of the
Church's conflict and victory in the later
Joshua. The final issue of the strife and
doom of the great spiritual enemy is seen
under the words, "The Lord will have war
with Amalek from generation to generation,"
and "the Lord said, I will utterly put out the
remembrance of Amalek from under heaven;"
while the mission of the Church as the divine
instrument of beneficence is set forth in those
often mistaken words of far-reaching prophecy,
"When the Lord thy God hath given thee
rest from all thine enemies round about,
in the land which the Lord thy God
giveth thee for an inheritance to possess it,
thou shalt blot out the remembrance of

Amalek from under heaven ; thou shalt not forget it."

We use the term beneficence advisedly. The Old Testament, it must be remembered, represents transactions which though upon a small stage are vast and universal in meaning. The Church described there is not a branch, but in fact the whole visible Church on earth in its organisation and early contraction, and, further, it is the type of that whole Church in its later expansion. It was less than any Church now in the value of its privileges, yet it was more than any now in the area of its meanings. Being a representation of the entire plan, God is properly present with it, and His dealings in it properly take the full and final character, which is to attend the ultimate consummation of His work. If that final crisis is to be a retributive application not only of mercy but also of strict judgments, then such unflinching judgments ought to be found in some way described among the incidents of the Old Testament, and were they omitted there the narrative would be inconsistent and incomplete.

In the New Testament the case is different. The Church there is no longer a defined outer system, with geographical boundaries and strict historical incidents; it is internally spread through many political systems of various form. Its work is much wider and deeper, but it has not the same condensed significance. The final issues now are more remote; the scale of the plan has become too vast to admit of their appearing on the narrow platform of time. Decision and retribution are not, however, on that account done away. They are still as strict, as just, as overwhelming in the forewarnings of the New Testament as they are in the actual occurrences of the Old. It might even be said they are more so.

There is thus a perfect harmony in the fundamental method of the two revelations. The difference is that the sanctions in the smaller Church are properly carried out at once in the present, while in the larger Church they are with the same propriety held back until the " fulness of time " in the future. In both God is sovereign. In both He says, "judgment is mine, I will repay," but the smallness of the field in the first case soon brings us to the issue; the wider extent in the second requires of us patience until the end shall be. It is not because the result at last will be different under the two Testaments that we are told not to avenge ourselves, and not to desire to do so, for the result in both cases will be similar. But it is because in the present advanced system it cannot be so fully said who is on the Lord's side as it could in the past one, since circumcision is now in the spirit and not in the flesh, and sonship is not tribal but mystical. We have neither the capacity nor commission for judgment as they then had; not because there will be no judgment, but because wheat and tares are mixed, and are to be now let grow together until the harvest.

It is probable that some persons who have reflected against the Old Testament on the ground of its severities may not have considered this point, but may have compared its books either with the temporary aspect of the New Testament instead of with its full and complete proposals, as should have been done.

Or else they may possibly have compared the Old Testament proceedings with floating sentiments drawn partly from beautiful maxims of the Gospel; partly from easy notions of society; and partly from benevolences of the natural world, and they may have considered the Book as failing in the comparison.

But even if we bring the matter with them to the common ground of affairs the Old Testament judgments seem unavoidable. The narrative we may note does not describe them as the willing act of the people. On the contrary, these take the side of the objector; and are adverse and remiss in carrying out severities pressed by God Himself. It was from this very circumstance that the whole nation was perpetually coming into misfortune, and that their leaders, as notably Saul, for sparing the Amalekite tribe, incurred the divine displeasure. It is not therefore the crude public sentiment of a barbarous age, which is by an unconscious dereliction of some true principles expressing itself in severities. Rulers and subjects are alike observed inclining to compromise, tolerance and lenity, and yielding

themselves, but unwilling instruments, to a
higher policy of severities they dislike.

These severities themselves, if we pass from
the first impulse of sentiment to a consideration
of reason, are evidently so useful that a truly
benevolent sentiment must itself at last approve
and agree with Scripture in requiring them.
It has been clearly and many times shown
that the people of Israel, and the system
entrusted to them, could not possibly without
such methods have been preserved in sufficient
integrity for the later work of the Holy Spirit
to rise on.   Without such periodical weedings
there could no more have grown up the
harvest of the Gospel than there could spring
crops of corn without clearings of the soil.

In accordance with the tenour of the Scripture
narrative we find that the teachings of secular
history, the experiences both of civil rule and
even also of the domestic circle, oblige us to
recognise that severities, prunings, and exci-
sions are at times necessary though austere
benevolences. Analogies of natural life, as
regards its preservations, restorations, and
cures, run the same way.   In short, the whole

judicial consensus of mankind requires that which their whole affectionate sentiment shrinks from. Nor is this conflict at variance with the tone of Scripture, but in the most direct agreement with it; so much so that the whole intricate mechanism of its plan may be seen working together, from first to last, to bring about by means of the Saviour, both in heavenly places and in the human estate, precisely that sort of compromise, compact, or balance, between the competing frames of justice and mercy, which we know to be in fact the practical question for ourselves to solve in our human affairs, and which we instinctively require to find reconciled in a truly divine plan.

While one great family of the desert was thus showing its hostility to the house of Jacob, another was approaching in friendship. Jethro, the chief of Midian, father-in-law to Moses, now came to him, together with Moses' wife and with her two sons. The narrative explains now a second time the meaning of the first son's name: " I have been an alien in a strange land," and adds the meaning of the second son's name, " the God of my father was my help, and delivered me from the sword of Pharaoh." These names had been given by Moses in his banishment. They were intended by him to commemorate his early trouble and deliverance. They equally express, it is now found, the wider transactions of his later fortunes. The training of the believer, and of all believers, run on the same line. The Church and the leader of the Church are one in probation and in triumph. This is still so from the beginning to the end.

After the circumcision in the flesh Moses' wife, with the children, had left him; now, after the baptism in the sea she returns and brings them with her, and the place of reunion is at the mount of God. There, at the beginning, God had foretold his people should come on their deliverance, and there was to be the point of contact between the departed.

Jethro sends to announce his arrival; Moses goes out to meet him; does him obeisance in reverence, and salutes him in love. He relates all that has happened. Then the priest of Midian glorifies the Lord, and makes this great

confession of faith, "now I know that the Lord
(the Jehovah, who is revealed to you, and who
is leading you) is greater than all Elohim." The
patriarchal priest then takes a burnt offering
and sacrifices peace offerings for God; and
after the sacrifice the elders of Israel came and,
as the narrative expressly informs us, Aaron at
their head, to partake of the sacrificial meal, at
which Jethro, the sacrificer, would be president.
On the morrow Jethro examines the arrangements of government; disapproves them;
offers his own advice and a patriarchal plan in
their stead, assuring Moses that if it is adopted
God shall be with him. Nor is he mistaken
in this; at a later period (see Deut. i.) it seems
with the divine approval to have been brought
before the people, and accepted as the national
system. After these circumstances, Moses lets
his father-in-law go, and Jethro returns to his
own land.

This whole transaction has been regarded
as an episode apart from the main stream of
the narrative. Whether the existence of such
episodes at all be consistent with the theory of
the Bible is not now the inquiry, but it can

hardly be considered in any case that this is one. Rather does this narrative of Jethro seem an important link in the organic system of Scripture. The fact, very prominent in his visit, is the superiority fully and willingly conceded to him. Though extraordinary condescensions of the Lord had raised Moses to the highest importance under a new dispensation just about to open, he yet at the commencement of it reverently owns allegiance to the patriarch of Midian, possessor and depository of the primitive faith. Nor is this owing merely to the ties of relationship between them, for in the next scene, where the name of Moses is kept back, and the action is placed in Aaron the future high-priest of Israel, and the elders who are at the time the religious representatives of the tribes, we have them all acting in subordination to the shepherd-prince of Midian, and after he has given in his allegiance to the Jehovah of the revelation, as identical with the Elohim of his own ancestral worship, we have him, and not either Aaron or the elders, taking the lead, offering sacrifices to God, and they all subordinately joining him in the sacramental feast.

This, in fact, amounts to the celebration of an alliance, and the outward recognition and cementing of a pact between two phases of the grand world-long religion, which is essentially one in the purposes of God. The patriarchal and the national thus visibly attach themselves together; and as at the beginning of the older system Abraham, in the hour of his greatest outer distinction, is brought for a moment into contact with a dimly seen representative of a still elder Church, so here Moses, after his victories, is also visited by an analogous character, one of whom little is known, except that he too, like Melchisidek, is a prince and a priest of the most high God. Like the more ancient the later visitant blesses God and blesses Israel, and while conferring a lasting benefit on the infant people by his advice he implants among them one of the great civil institutions of the patriarchs, tending more, perhaps, than anything else which could have been devised to perpetuate popular liberty, and to secure the future commonwealth.

Thus his visit is even on this side a demonstration in favour of the two general principles to be handed on—the recognition of the one Jehovah-God, and the reaction from the tyrannies of misrule. It occurs at the very spot and moment of time that the dispensation of the law is going to commence. It is as if a very ambassador from the patriarchal epoch of the past had been deputed to attend at the holy mount to testify, to initiate, to unite with them there in praise and sacrifice, and to hand over to the charge of the new agency the sacred deposit of their ancestors, the beginnings of religion now about to be expanded ; the beginnings of government now about to be advanced.

Nor does the matter stop at that point. Though we may regard it as an act of adhesion it is not to be considered an act of surrender on the part of the patriarchal. On the contrary, at the very moment the Hebrew was going to be raised to such a height of religious distinction it was impressed on the first page of his very credentials of covenant that God had other subjects besides the tribes, and a wider domain than Canaan; that the pleadings of sacrifice were not to be confined to the priesthood alone, but that outside the courses of Levi there might still be the blood of the lamb upon altars of acceptance.

Moses let his father-in-law depart to his own country. The system he was to inaugurate had not sufficiently wide invitations to retain him, but his very coming had been an indication that there were attractive powers hid away in it, and was already a suggestion of the final incorporation of the patriarchal and Mosaic in the future Messiah. At that present time an alliance of affinity between the two was all that could be effected. Each had to go its own way and carry forward its own mission; the patriarchal struggling to maintain the primitive outlines among the corruptions of the wide world; the Mosaic retracing and deepening those outlines within its distinctive fortress, and yet each, though working alone, working still in relation; the Hebrew sending out missions; the patriarchal sending in converts; the Hebrew providing the motive impulse; the patriarchal preparing the ground for reception and response. An incident was wanted at such a critical moment to express these essential characteristics of the plan. The (so-called) episode of Jethro has supplied it with admirable propriety.

CHAPTER IX.

THE country from the sea up to Sinai has been happily described as rising level above level, like steps leading to a natural sanctuary. A traditional reverence is said to have already attached to the mountain and to the district, which the Egyptians regarded as in a measure sacred. The declaration of God Himself had now made it "holy ground." At this special spot, at a special crisis of time, Israel arrived and camped before the mount. Moses had known from the first that the people were there to do service to Jehovah, and had understood it to be a service of sacrificial worship (Exod. v. 3). He now goes forward in advance of his people; ascends into this natural temple, and the Lord speaks in it.

The prospect of the nation is in the very first words widely extended. The missionary thought, with which Abraham's career commenced, is now in an advanced form placed at once before his descendants at the beginning of their national existence. In Abraham, the prophet, all the nations of the earth were to be blessed. The " house of Jacob " now is to be a dynasty of priests, consecrated for " the other sheep not of their fold," the flock of the whole world. The entire nation is to be holy and ministerial. By obedience to the divine voice as it should speak from time to time, and by keeping the divine covenant, now once for all to be entered into, Abraham's descendants, his seed, are to begin to be a blessing to all Jehovah's earth. The master idea of the work, which no nation would then have conceived or cared to carry out, is thus once again provided for. The people are officially assembled; they have the matter fully laid before them ; they all accept the prerogative and duty. Moses returns their words to the Lord.

The divine terms and conditions of covenant having now to be made known in rules, their God will give these in such a direct way that it shall never be doubted in Israel they are from Him. For this purpose they must come up to the sanctuary mount. Before approaching

a place hallowed by the divine presence preparation is necessary. They are accordingly
purified for a marked time, and on the third
day, being regarded as clean, they are led
forward. But as they are to go to what is in
reality a most sacred temple, here, as in other
temples, a limit is fixed, beyond which
encroachment would be sacrilege. On the
third day the Lord descends in emblematic fire
on the mount, suddenly visiting His temple,
and Moses, the mediator of the time, with the
future high-priest Aaron, is summoned up to
the higher and more intimate sanctuary.

The covenant conditions, by keeping which
Israel is to carry on its priestly nationality for
the world, are now announced by God, and
under a candid examination they are seen to be
admirably fitted to advance the great purpose.
They are in ten clauses (or " words ") cardinal
principles absolutely complete, yet capable
under one aspect of being still further condensed ; capable under another of widest
expansion. The first quality is implied
in their being given in two tables; the
second is seen by their re-appearance in

the more copious "judgments" immediately following.

At the first division of the words the thought is turned up to the mount, where Jehovah is; where, though He is, He is unseen; where He is in His reverend majesty. With the mind thus fixed on the mount, the mandates to worship none but Him; to worship Him by no visible images; to reverence His name, commend themselves at once to the Hebrew as self-evidently right, and from them flows out a further moral propriety and need, introducing the systematic devotion of the fourth command.

At the second division of the "words" the thought returns from the mount to the camp. It begins inside the tent with the law of the home; respect for the authority whose necessary charge and care is the happiness, security, and well-doing of the paternal tent. This is the fifth word. The thought passes out from this paternal tent to the tents of neighbours around; the domestic happiness, the safety, the possessions, the good repute of those surrounding dwellings are to be respected and cared for as well. They also are homes, and home being now sanctified all homes are sacred. He, who as a priestly man, has just been looking up to the mount of God, and who now is looking below upon the tent which is his own dwelling, and on the tents of the priestly nation, pitched beside his own, will feel the commands which secure these, viz., the sixth, seventh, eighth, and ninth binding at once ; he will feel it instinctively and without moral strain ; and, further, he will pass on from them naturally to that final principle which guards the " words " at this end, even as the first command guarded them at the other, and he will not desire in heart that which is forbidden in action.

Thus the covenant is not even in appearance arbitrary, and the Hebrews would not be able to help observing that it is righteous in fullest and most practical equity, as their God intended they should do. It is a characteristic of true religion that it grows out of circumstance in its revelation, even as in its application to individuals it adapts itself gradually in the gradual growth of the life. There is a wonderful cohesion and completeness in the "words," which the more they are examined will the more appear. Yet while the rules themselves rise out in lasting and complete equality, a systematic whole which cannot be altered or improved, still, for the time, an emphasis is laid on points where temporary danger would be greatest, and this is introduced by an appeal to their own experience, " ye have seen that I have talked with you from heaven," therefore " ye shall not make with me gods of silver, neither shall ye make unto you gods of gold."

The qualities of the commandments have appeared admirable, even to those who reject their divine origin, and attribute them only to a very wonderful man. One of these writers piles up marvels on the point. They have, he says, " an incomparable value," " a remarkable influence." " They restrict themselves to eternal truths, as if they had descended from heaven." They are " the most indispensable and comprehensive propositions;" " as judiciously selected as skilfully arranged;" they show in this arrangement " the same master-mind which had before it the profound truths of the whole law." "There is a skilful grouping," "a natural sequence," "a wise ordaining," so that "nothing can be more excellent and more unique than these commandments of the tables of stone, both in their contents and their arrangement." They, and indeed the whole idea of the law, furnish "the few and mighty impulses which from that time forward incessantly acted in ever-widening circles, and with ever-increasing result." In short, "they constitute in themselves such a distinct and well-connected whole, that we cannot but confess"—what?—"that in their original unity they must have proceeded from one great creative spirit"—and then we are dropped to the most limping anti-climax ; the great creative spirit turns out to be only some remarkable man, "springing, like Pallas, at once fully armed from the head of Zeus."

Here, again, are difficulties gratuitously brought in quite equal at least to those they are intended to do away, and to escape a wonder consistently accredited, benevolent in aspect, and of proved benefit, we are asked to accept another wonder, embarrassed with circumstantial difficulties, of limited and constrained intentions, and which when believed in has always done its supporters far more harm than good. More than this, in the name of philosophy we are asked to discard the most sublime organisation of ethics, and for the sake of supplanting it by a pedestrian theory, without due balance, association, or sanctions, enthusiastic, if not deceptive, in its origin—an origin commendable only on assumptions which shake the very bases of right and wrong.

Taking worship of the one Jehovah as the motive thought of the first table and reverence of parents as the point of departure for the second, and regarding each of them as the original idea from which the other commands of the two tables, respectively, arise and take occasion, we thus have in this fundamental compact a distinct promulgation of the two great primary principles and projects, running through the plan; one, the restoration of mankind from idolatry, and their progressive advance to a full service and knowledge of God, progressively made known to them in His paternal attributes and requirements; the other, their recovery from the ancient tyrannies and the gradual reconstitution of society upon the equitable and kindly basis of the paternal or family method, so that, however vast and complex civil organisations might in the future become, there should still be within them the prevailing principle of fraternal regard and affection with which society commenced, and in which it is at last to find its complete prosperity and happiness under the headship of our one God and Father, and the brotherhood of the one Lord and Saviour, Jesus Christ, in whom the Law will at last find its complete fulfilments, and who Himself declared and showed how it might all be resolved back to these two heads.

Nor was this all that was done at the great crisis of Moses. Not only, as we have seen, was there wanted, then and always, a true constructive plan and process for religion and society, but further there was also a want no less imperative—more urgent, indeed, than any other—the want of that ministration of pardoning and healing, which should render the soul capable of taking its place by

true citizenship in renovated religion and
society. Not only, therefore, ought we to
have, in a law really promulgated from
heaven, announcements of duty to God and
man, announcements which however comprehensive and beautifully fit would not be all
the soul would be yearning to receive, but we
should also have that merciful medicative
process, which a really divine sympathy would
know to be our deepest and first want, even
before we ourselves could identify, so as to
frame it in expression.

Surrounding the law, therefore, as the
bounds environed Sinai, bringing up in contact
with its truths while preserving from its risks,
we want to have everywhere expressions of
the redemption which alone places a ransomed
people in a position to listen and obey. It
was then a magnificent stroke of the narration,
far beyond the previsions of an ancient scribe,
which brought together the whole world in
representation at the threshold of Sinai, to
offer there together that worship which had
already been introduced by its patriarchal
correlative, the accepted Jethro sacrifice. It

may be with a fitness of suggestion, less striking because only a suggestion, but not less really wonderful, that we find placed between the "words" and the "judgments"—between the principles of law and the applications of law—instructions for the altar, and which teach that as there is to be one Jehovah God unseen, to whom in heaven worship is to go up unimpeded by earthly symbols, so there is to be one altar on which sacrifice to Him is to be offered, and that this altar is still, in their new splendid worship, to be kept the same plain construction of earth or rough rock which their fathers had always used; at which Abraham had offered and Isaac had been bound; thus, in this essential of worship, preserving in the most palpable way the unity of the old and the new; showing that the rite was to have the same meaning now as then, and also that though it was to have fresh elaborations it was not yet susceptible of increased value; still preserving it as a central requisite; still retaining it as the spot and method of acceptance and of entrance to duty and peace; still keeping ready, if we may so say, in its unimpaired simplicity of grandeur, the platform of Calvary itself.

From the "words," the living fountains of law, the revelation passes after the dividing mark of the sacrificial to the "judgments," the applied principles of law, and as (in Exod. xii. 44) the first thought, after providing the paschal lamb, was to provide for the slave's partaking of it, thus striking the home note of spiritual and temporal freedom; so here, after the rule of the altar and the attendant promise of divine presence and blessing, the first provision of the judgments is for the recovery of liberty by the slave; a fact, like the other, full of significance, and in strict accordance with the underlying meaning of the Scripture work, which is essentially to deliver from bondage, and to secure in the "glorious liberty" of children under the covenant.

The two tables of the "words" are to lie in the ark, as the two rules of Jesus are to rest in the heart, but the applications or "judgments" being for outer use take here a public form, and follow the outline usual in municipal law—protection of person, property, morality, and repute. But there are mixed in with them distinctive features, peculiar in themselves, yet explicable by reference to the purposes of the system, with which they are in complete harmony. A blow to the parent as the root of violence, and breach of the root-law of the second table is a capital offence. A sacrifice to idols as a breach of the root-law of the first table, the beginning of immorality, and the first of thefts is also a capital offence.

On the other hand, exceptions of mercy in favour of the weak, and generosities of self-denial, unusual in the strict generalisation and lower morality of other legislations, find an appropriate place in this paternal code, and are guarded and invigorated by the exercises of unselfishness enjoined in the devotion of first fruits, and those surrenders implied in the graduated Sabbatical rests. The three feasts provide for the periodical assembly of the national family, with their tribute to their God, round the central altar; and, again (Exod. xxiii. 18), the thought of the blood of the sacrifice, and the acceptable way of presenting it, bring on the close of the series. A final warning to obedience and allegiance, together with a final promise of success and blessing, conditional on them, follow, and the "judgments" close.

The Lord having now declared generally, in the "words" for perpetual adherence, and specially in the "judgments," as the application and conditioning of the general, what are His terms of entering into covenant, invites Moses to bring representatives of the whole nation up into His sanctuary, that, on their acceptance, they may there enjoy the privilege of closer worship, to which, as the covenant people, they will be entitled. Moses accordingly comes down to the Hebrews, tells them all the "words," and all the "judgments," and they proclaim with one voice their acceptance of the terms. Moses now puts these terms in writing, builds an altar, and causes burnt-offerings and peace-offerings to be sacrificed to the Lord on behalf of the whole people, who are expressed as being fully present by twelve piles or pillars, raised up by or round the altar.

The occasion of the sacrifice is peculiar. It

is an admission of all into a closer holier union with God, described for the understanding of the time as admission into a priestly caste. It therefore fitly has resemblances to the subsequent admission of the official priests into their office, and to the re-admission of the excluded leper into the holy community, and there will be found analogies running generally through the narrative between the duty, the offendings, and the punishments of the national and the official priesthoods. In this sacrifice half of the blood was sprinkled on the altar, and half of it on the people, after the writing of the Law had been read aloud to them, and they had given their promise and consent to it.

In sacrifice there ever resided, *i.e.*, in the acceptance of God, the meaning of atonement. Here the inner thought seems that as completely as the blood of atonement was offered and presented before God, so also, in proportionate completeness, was that blood's value applied to His people. It shows forth those correlations of human and divine action which have their meeting-place in sacrament. It is

EE

an intermediate expression of the blessed truth of salvation, never departed from, which appears at one end of the scheme, on the door-posts in Egypt, as deliverance from death, and at the other, in the apocalypse, as eternal life, on the robes "washed and made white in the blood of the Lamb." It is a special modification of Hebrew sacrament, but one conveying, as all sacrament, the complement of all sacrifice—answering grace from Him who accepts and therefore blesses.

The transaction being complete, the representatives of the tribes go up into the sanctuary mount; an apparition of Him who is now the covenant God of Israel, who is prince of God, is vouchsafed to them, and they eat, unharmed, the sacrificial meal of their covenant.

But from this point, to which the Church has been allowed to penetrate, the typical mediator is specially summoned into a still higher place—holy of holies—even as the divine antitype, after the renewed law and the new covenant, sealed in His blood, left His people awhile. Moses, like Him, in departing gave the charge to occupy till he came, and, ascending up, a cloud received him out of their sight. He left behind authority in Aaron and Hur, representing the civil power and the priestly, and for forty days (the time expressing a completed epoch), he was withdrawn from his people. It was good it should be so soon expressed in figure to man's impatience that such absences are part of the economy of grace.* In the meantime his absence was fruitful. He had, in a sense, gone to prepare a place for them. He was receiving in heavenly places instructions for a tabernacle, which would be on earth a type of heavenly things themselves.

---

* Cyprian, De Bono Patientiæ.

CHAPTER X.

THE Mosaic revelation has consistent methods
running through its whole course. It ever
regards person, place, and time. The abstract
form in which philosophies are cast show them
dependent on mind, but a divine system will
naturally move among events, for action itself
is a divine word and a method of expression
which, though inaccessible to philosophies, is
far more complete. The free play of incident
in the system of Moses is itself therefore a
badge of authority, and the constant transitions
by which verbal and active expressions carry
forward its progress speak of its divine origin.

The movement of the plan, again, is not
merely regulative; it is incessantly action in
advance. There is a place to go to, a time to
go in, and a man to lead. A Canaan paradise
land, tasted, lost, and to be possessed once
more, and this according to a promise from
the first. There is a single leader; a man of
sorrows; alone in conflict; alone in the burden

of the people; rejected yet successful; priest before the priests, prophet, lawgiver and king.

There is further a time, meted out in parcels; four hundred years, then forty years three times repeated, and generally a course of slow progressions, leading up to crises according with what may be seen in nature itself. The same sort of sympathy through trial, which the Epistle to the Hebrews declares to exist between Christ and his people, was here to be seen in Christ's forerunner. In his fortieth year Moses, by a quick movement, was committed to the cause of Israel. After the trials of another forty years he was really trained for success in their cause. An experience, similar to their chief's, was about to befall the community, and events were to show that, after their first pledge of allegiance, forty years among solemn associations would still be necessary before Israel could enter into the land which was to be at once rest from the past and also the beginning of wider activities in the future. The long passage of trial had fitted Moses for his work with Israel, and the corresponding probation would enable Israel to leave its lesson for the world. Such waitings and movements, and among such circumstances, may have been valuable conditions by which the human mind could lay hold firmly of the truths of divine unity and government.

Sinai itself was at once a sacred and a central site; indeed the two terms are in a degree identical, for whatever is sacred must be central. The one head of the people, Moses, had first stood there alone, and there had held converse with God. Now the whole people were before it. To them, and to the world through them, the doings at Sinai were to be a sort of re-entry to Paradise, and that in a substantial sense, and the place itself a "very gate of heaven."

Adam originally had a law, the germ of all law; "quasi matrix omnium præceptorum Dei." "In it," says Tertullian, "we recognise all the precepts enclosed which afterwards cropped up, given through Moses."* It was already the ten words; already the two tables; the love of God and man. The breaking of

* Tertullian. Adversus Judæos. II.

it threw our parents out of Paradise, not by
arbitrary penalty, but by needed consequence
and evil worked on to destruction in the
deluge. Sacred history had hitherto been a
slow travelling back towards the lost centre·
Obedience regained a position in the perfect
offering of Noah, and in the accepted sacrifice
secured the promise of preservation. Around
the sacrifices of Abraham were again grouped
advancing prospects, and at his great surrender
of love in not withholding his only begotten son,
the point of Eve is touched, "Thy seed shall
possess the gate of his enemies," and advanced
in definition to—"In thy seed shall all the
nations of the earth be blessed." And now
the people, already themselves a fulfilment
in first-fruit—numerous, victorious over the
enemy, and to be victorious again—stand at
the door of Sinai, listen to the law of Paradise, and pledge themselves to obedience, not
simply but in the solemnities and safeguards of
the blood of sacrifice, answering with one
voice, "all the words which the Lord hath
said will we do."

The value and import of this answer is not

to be measured by the shortness of their performance, but by the spiritual height of Sinai and length from Egypt; by the presence of Jehovah; by the donation of the rule; by the action of the mediator; and by the blood-sprinkling which had passed on to both the divine and the human side. It was a pledge to do what Adam failed in doing; to reverse his decision, and to take up again in an extended form the work he had dropped. This offering of allegiance indeed was but little, yet it offered Israel's best in God's appointed manner and accepted time, and it therefore placed man once again, and more fully than in any past period, at the re-entrance of Paradise. It in itself, in one sense, constituted a sort of re-entry into lost privilege.

But that was not all; as the law of God was now to be distinctly over, so also the presence of God was to be now discernably with him, which was another quality of Paradise lost at the fall. Noah had been found righteous, and Abraham an orderer of his house in obedience, and God had spoken and blessed; but now the nation was in covenant, and had surrendered to God the best in man, in obedience to His gracious summons. The whole Paradise law was set out for them, and accepted in extensions of form and meaning. Thus one great restoration of the past was gained, and gained in the best form, by an advance towards a future. But what would such a law, so laid down, have been had it remained alone? Did not its very donation mean Divine presence, commerce, and communion? The love of its first table is the love of a Being near and not far off. The love of its second is a fraternity in relation to Him; the love of a family around its head. Divine presence, therefore, now becomes a pressing requisite of the theory.

We have, then, various movements of thought testifying the same way, and soliciting a manifestation of Divine presence. If we believe a law was given in Paradise, there broken, and man in consequence expelled from the presence of God, until then enjoyed, and if we go on to believe that law now to have been again restored, the expectation necessarily follows that the presence of God

would be restored as well; restored in complex fulness, since the law was both complex
and full; by means of a mediator, since the
law was in the hands of a mediator, and
surrounded by confessions and cleansings of
sin, since in such vouchsafed presence sin
must be incessantly purged.

Again, if we accept as true that this Israel
came out of Egypt, where the fable gods were
considered to live among the people in shrines,
central and accessible, and there to speak and
reply; if we further accept it that this Israel
believed themselves brought out by a God
shown a stronger and more present help in
trouble than the other divinities; that Israel
considered itself led by Him, following Him in
action and clustering round Him in rest, can
we suppose they would have been satisfied,
safe, or powerful for good, without His manifested presence among them—a presence they
must certainly have expected, desired, and felt
necessary? Or, once more, if we allow this to
have been no narrow scheme, but a movement
intended to influence the world, was not a real
donation of what all men not unreasonably

desired, the very way to impress them most widely?

Nor should this be objected to as incompatible with God's proceedings, for whatever ideas we may please to frame of the powers and fit attributes of the Divine Being, we ought at least to reserve for Him this special prerogative—the right of progressively accommodating His conduct to the progressing phases of man's inner history—a history in some considerable measure influenced by Himself; and of speaking and acting in sundry times in diverse manners as the wants of His creatures might require. A man may move alone, but a child needs a constant presence. It is the means not only of security but also of instruction and advance. We do not wonder, then, but it commends itself as an authentic utterance when directly the covenant is complete we read— "Let them make me a sanctuary, that I may dwell among them;" and when we find the reason of it, "I will dwell among the children of Israel, and they shall know that I am the Lord their God;" and when we find it described as Jehovah's very purpose in the Exodus, that He brought them forth out of the land of Egypt, that He might dwell among them. The special presence in restrained type with the one nation, being a preliminary of the special presence, in unreserved donation to all nations, by the Holy Spirit in the Gospel, which is the fulfilment of the promise first made to Abraham.

The hollow square then in the centre of the tents required a chief tent for the presence of the Lord, and He, whose voice in the first Paradise, had been heard walking in the garden in the cool of the day, and who was then hidden from by the disobedient, was now again with His children, and now again made His promise to their beginnings of obedience—"I will set my tabernacle among you, and will walk among you, and will be your God, and ye shall be my people."

It is very likely that a completer view of psychology may show a revealed presence of God necessary for the very construction of the religious idea, and there are already strong tendencies that way. As regards Judaism in particular there is no reasonable method of explaining the previous narrative, or the crisis of Moses itself, if we ignore this fact of a revealed presence. Most ingenious speculators are driven to the greatest straits, and in explaining away the results which we believe to come necessarily from this presence of God they invite us to the belief of things much more unlikely. Thus Ewald would have us suppose that the "fundamental thought, the corner-stone of every true religion," viz., "the knowledge of the true deliverer," came to these Israelites alone of all men, and to them in consequence of their deep distress, and that "they sprung up from their despair, and so were the first to become conscious of the might and eternity of man's spirit, and of the true God its eternal refuge." He goes on to say that this "real God, who created the world and works in it, is truly kindred but infinitely superior to us, and that he calls to himself and seeks to deliver his image and noblest creature—man;" "but that man only is delivered by the Divine grace, preventing and calling him, who by his own spirit

enters into this eternal spirit." That when
once the whole of this fundamental thought
has arisen in one place it can never again
perish, but must go on, and in the end over-
throw every opposition in the world. That
"in all the nations there had not been as yet
a single individual who had grasped this idea,
or who was willing to take it for his guide."
That Moses was the one man who "had a
wonderful divine work to do," by laying hold of
this " astonishing new thought," and that "no
earthly power could frustrate the eternal
destiny of a spirit which had this work to do
on earth."

It is in one sense a comforting yet in another
a very chastening lesson for all, when we
witness the difficulty into which the brightest
intelligence is at once thrown in its efforts to
cast aside the plain revelation of Scripture,
and while rejecting God's way in it to retain
God's gifts by it. How totally inconsistent is
it, for instance, with the facts set out, to say
that Israel was by the very depth of their
distress, first illuminated with the idea of the
might of man's spirit and of God as its refuge.

We see all through the account that nothing of the sort was the case, but that instead of being a great people, leaping up to lay hold on a high abstraction, they were a very depressed community, constantly declining, craving, and leaning to sense, and with difficulty led along at all.

Why, too, are we to concede so arbitrary a supposition as that in "that time under Moses infinite truth first cast its bright beam upon the earth?" Had there not been before then many deep and bitter distresses among men? Why, if the causation at work be only natural, should sorrow never until then have had on the heart the effect sorrow was appointed to produce? Why, if the spirit, not of the Hebrew only, but of all men, be as described, thus "mighty" and "truly kindred to God"— why should this supposed appointed means of revelation, deep distress, have failed to move the vast mass of sufferers, and yet have produced such an extraordinary effect on a particular handful, "that they would never allow the result to be taken from them?" And why, if this handful were so superior as assumed (though the assumption is against the facts), and if, as affirmed, the Mosaic includes within it the Christian, "realised through the inherent germinating force of the fundamental idea which then arose, and in its own time necessarily led to it"—why is it that the Jews have so steadily refused to advance and embrace this Christianity, but remain still outside, misunderstanding both their own position and where it should lead them to, thus being both the only persons who could grasp the grand idea, and also the only ones who could not follow it out?

Many such questions might be put, but we will only add one more remark, viz., that it is hardly a generous or dignified conception of the Eternal, to describe Him in one sentence as omnipotent, and as deeply interested in man, and then to go on to describe Him in the next as inflicting distresses, or permitting them through many long generations, and yet not able Himself to initiate relief, but obliged to wait for truth and comfort to come to his creatures, until the very pressure of afflictions had enabled a few of them suddenly to leap up and touch the idea of Him in their despair, and by slow degrees pass this idea on to the rest of mankind. Why should man with an incessant real want never get a real supply? Why with a true nature should he be doomed in his highest desires to gain but untruths? For who will persuade us by subtle refinings that a picture we paint is a real person really answering and having more in it than we ourselves put there? Law of nature is the supposed obstacle to divine benevolence in this. If so, nature would itself become the divine, and a harsh divinity too, instead of the clement benefactress we find her. But the first law of nature is a ministration by God to His creatures, adjusted to the character He has given them, and a ready and real supply of our reasonable want. And what want more pressing, we ask, than the want of our souls?

Infinitely grander, more advanced and, even before evidence, nearer to the truth seem to come the descriptions of the Bible, showing a God revealing Himself at the very first sorrow of the first sinner, never deserting His Church, but incessantly with mankind in increasing

GG

revelation from the patriarchal altars, through
the tabernacle and temple, on to the upper
room of the Apostles, and giving Himself
incessantly in increasing brightness and fulness,
only restrained in His devotion by our failing
capacity to receive, and ever active and effectual in making each truth told, and each
manifestation shown, a ground of further
advance; never stopping from any stint on
His side, but only waiting to bring us on;
ever widening His circle of impression; from
the first aiming at and effecting improvements
outside the tribes, and seeking to draw man's
spirit on to a love and liberality to others,
wide in accordance with His own; a God not
sought out but seeking ; " afflicted in all His
people's afflictions, the angel of His presence
saving them; in His love and His pity
redeeming them ; and bearing and carrying
them all the days of old."

But to return; accepting the truth of the
manifested divine presence, so invaluable, and
perhaps so demonstrably essential, for any
approach to an actual theosophy, we now find
ourselves at this point; where the first man had

stood alone there now the whole people were standing together at the Sinai paradise ground. The law to the one had been but a single command, within which more lay hid; to them the law was now a code in extension; a code not only given but also accepted in the covenant blood. Still, however, bounds kept them out from the inner paradise, and their privilege was but initial. Only the chiefs of religion and civil life once in sacrament;· only the mediator of the present, Moses ; only the mediator of the future, Joshua; could enter up within. But though man could not go up, God would come down and dwell with men, and be in their midst the centre, leader, and inspirer of their life. Thus even the historical cast of the transactions was itself a grand expression of Gospel purposes, showing beforehand the work of Jesus; both His leading out His people; the covenant in His blood; His ascent into heaven, and the consequent indwelling of God the Holy Ghost in the hearts of His people. The whole bringing great restorations in religion and life here, and bringing to Canaan when the wilderness is over.

Nor was this all. We shall presently see that the sanctuary itself, made after patterns given in the mount, and so professedly expressive of divine purpose, was filled in all its parts, and attendant particulars of rite, with echoes and reflections of the same truths, and that while for the times then present it served wonderfully the wants of the people, both for the policies of organisation round its centre and for their training in knowledge of sin and purity, it yet further, and beyond the Israel of that day, had full Gospel meanings for the Israel of Grace, and set out in beautiful harmonies of figure precious realities already moving in heavenly places, and gradually to be revealed in time.

Such a method of proceeding, if it can be substantiated, at once declares a divine hand, and stamps the system as from above. If it can be shown even probably to exist it claims the most close and devout scrutiny of its pretensions. The Scripture takes up grounds of this anticipatory sort, and fairly rests much on them. In Isaiah the argument is insisted on in three successive chapters,* Jehovah

* xliv., 7 ; xlv., 21 ; xlvi., 10.

asserting Himself as on Sinai, and claiming to
be believed in as the only God, since He alone
can "appoint the ancient people," "set in
order the things that are coming," "declaring
the end from the beginning, and from ancient
times the things that are not yet done." And
indeed, the prefigurements by type are even
more gratifying, if possible, in this respect, than
those by prophecy, for prophecy by its method of
expression, directs attention and tends in some
measure to attract conformity, but the type
contains the truth silently embedded, and till
events have come forth it is not seen how
exact an impress of them was long before
hieroglyphed on the structures of ancient
polity and religion.

Moses now "gat him up into the mount;
and Moses was in the mount forty days and
forty nights." The Lord spake unto him
there, giving exact directions, and showing the
pattern of the tabernacle and all its instruments. From the offerings of the people he
was to take materials, and first to make an
ark, in which he was to place "the testimony" (*i.e.*, the record on stone of the law of

the ten "words") which the Lord would give him. Then he was to make a mercy seat, with cherubim, and place it upon the ark, the testimony being inside. This was the first essential.

After this Moses was to make a special table, "to set upon it shew bread before the Lord alway." Next he was to make a golden candlestick, a shaft and six branches, seven lamps in all, and "look thou make them after their pattern, which was shewed thee in the mount." The making of these three things being provided for with exact and minute care, next are given particular instructions for every detail of the curtains and boarding of the tent which was to contain them, and "thou shalt rear up the tabernacle according to the fashion thereof, which was shewed thee in the mount."

Then he was to make a veil to divide between "the holy place and the most holy," and to place the mercy seat upon the ark in the most holy place within the veil, and then outside the veil he was to set the table on the north side, and the candlestick over against it on the south side. Then he was to make hangings for the door of the tabernacle, to enclose it and its contents within it. At this point is completed the first idea of the tabernacle, and the subject passes on to matters outside. It will be observed that the incense altar had not yet been named, but occurs later in another relationship.

Scripture indicates that both in the above and in other incidents a whole system of typically figured truths lies embedded. Nor, indeed, is this more than would be expected. As soon as it is once allowed that the Almighty did, in fact, reveal to the one community, on behalf of the entire human race, with most minute particularity of detail and pattern, and under circumstances of impressive dignity, a series of directions for the conduct and machinery of worship, enjoining very strict adherence to them, so soon the inference almost necessarily arises that those directions must have wider and deeper connections than appear on their surface.

The question is how shall these connections be put together? We have in the New

Testament sufficiently definite explanations of the older types to lay open the beginnings of a scale and system of interpretation. The extent to which we may apply this has always been a controversy. On the one hand it has been attempted to confine the province of typology to those Old Testament incidents, which are interpreted in Scripture itself as types; on the other hand an effort has been made to extend it over the whole surface of the Bible, thus making every part of its development in time a shadow or reflection of the transactions of the eternal world. That some such relation as this may exist is very possible, and indeed to some of us will appear very likely, but the more just choice for ourselves would seem to be to accept the Scripture-interpreted types as a key by which to regulate the value of other related transactions in scale with them; not on the one hand refusing to use them as fruitful of suggestions, not on the other pressing their suggestiveness outside the group and connections to which they belong.

In applying this mixed method, since interpretations of almost all writers more or less vary, some liberty remains to each of us, and it may be a more useful contribution, without attempting dogmatism, to suggest our own impressions rather than to aim at accommodation with a variety of theories more or less at variance among themselves.

We should begin by remembering that the patriarchal history shows the "ten words" not to be new inventions but old rules, understood and in action among the earlier beginnings of society, and now, under Moses, promulgated afresh with emphatic sanctions. This is so surely true of most of them that it becomes probably true of the remainder, and thus, for instance, one of the strongest inferences for a primeval Sabbath is, that the rule of the Sabbath has place by the side of the other laws in the tables.

As these rules are not new so again they are not arbitrary. Far otherwise; they are on reflection seen to be conditions necessary for restoring an interrupted communication with the divine; not accidentals but essentials for a true religion and life. A " word " of God

is, in a sense, then, a living power ; a sort of
presence of God; a preparation for the presence of "The Word;" properly, therefore,
given immediately by God to man, from mouth
to mouth, and from hand to hand; regarded
as the centre of the older revelation, and
placed in its ark and innermost shrine. , And,
going forth from that sanctuary, this essential
gift was to spread itself out over the whole life
of the people, both secular and religious, by
means of the applied law, saturating that life
in all its incidents, and sanctifying it even as
Israel was baptised unto Moses in the cloud.

The divine law in its essence is the divine
will, and where the divine will is revealed there
the Divine is, and a perfect acceptance and
absorption of the law, and identification of self
with it, and life in absolute accordance and
submission to it would mean in other words
this—the presence of the Divine Spirit, in
continuing possession and power in and over
the inner life. Had it therefore been possible
to frame a law which should have been both
fully expressive of the Divine, and which also
could have been fully accepted and obeyed by

men, such might possibly have been the way of salvation. But that, alas! could never happen among us, for "the law" which, being in essence divine, cannot deflect from its truth, "is spiritual, but we are carnal, sold under sin," and so, though itself holy and just, and good, it meets in the members another law warring with it. And this depravation is universally admitted in the very structure of all human laws, which are aimed merely to be preventive and remedial, leaving good to be its own reward. Theorists, too, are clearly convinced of this. Thus Locke, after picturing what he calls a natural state of society, fancies that we were quickly driven from it to laws and government "by the corruption and degeneracy of men."*

The commandment, therefore, though ordained to life, could not give "life and peace," "in that it was weak through the flesh," and the devout soul found it writing against him sentences of death, and these pains and convictions of conscience brought in by means of the Law, that is both by its deeper principles

* 'On Government,' II., 9.

and by its plain applications in their society, shewed them disease, and called for and caused them to cast about for its remedy; which remedy sacrificial offerings provided in a way for the time then being, and "therefore almost all things are by the law purged by blood, and without shedding of blood, is no remission." That is to say, these "patterns of things in the heavens," which were shown to Moses in the mount, were purified with a pattern of the actual sacrifice. They being constantly offered in typical expiation of the sins of the people, expressed beforehand the eternal transaction by which "Christ was offered to bear the sins of many."

The law, then, being thus in its essence divine—being indeed in a sense a divine presence, as well as power, among them—should properly occupy the first and central place in their system, assuming that system to be really itself divine. The Hebrew arrangements, therefore, at this point exactly fulfil the needed requirements.

Again, the true and final dwelling place of the divine in law being not in the book of

precise legislative enactment, which, while a
conduit, is a limitation and restraint of its
energies, but in the conscience and inner life,
cardinal principles, and not codified rules,
should be the essential primary expression of
it. This requirement, also, we find is met in
the Hebrew system. Further, it is conceivable that there may be still more delicate
and deeper truths, requiring delineation and
finding it in the incidents of this transaction. If law to be a vital saving power,
require to be impressed by God Himself,
and not merely upon the external but in
the very inner nature, then the circumstance
of the principles of the law of twofold duty
being written in the material tables by the
very personal contact of God may be deeply
significant, and it may even be possible that
the doubling of this circumstance by so giving
the tables twice, may reflect the facts of the
law first so given to Adam, and broken at the
very threshold of society, and then a second
time given again upon tables provided from
the humanity of Jesus, and written in and
filled by the Spirit.

And the same may be further shadowed, or first expressed in a higher phase by this law dwelling incessantly in an ark, which ark was to be made the first thing of all, and to come from man's side as the law did from God's, and to be beautified with decorations of worth and purity, and this material receptacle, and the divine law ever resident within it, were to be taken into the very holiest place of all, even as Jesus Christ himself is gone into the heavens, and in every typical march and movement it was not the law nor the ark, but the ark with the law in it, as one united presentment, which was to head them, even as in all progression of the Church, we believe ourselves headed by the divine, contained in the personality and incorporated with the humanity of Jesus Christ.

The question next arises whether we are to regard the mercy seat as distinct from, or as completing the idea of the ark, and the Scripture leads us to adopt the latter view. In Exodus xl. 3, Moses is only told to put in the inner tabernacle "the ark of the testimony," but in verse 20-21, we find that in obeying this he "put the testimony into the ark, and put the mercy seat above upon the ark, and he brought the ark into the tabernacle." Again, when the opposite process is going on in Numbers iv. 5, we have, "they shall take down the covering veil and cover the ark of testimony with it." The mercy seat then appears to be treated as part of the idea of the ark.

In interpreting the mercy seat in accordance with the above scale, it may possibly be regarded as expressing the sacrificial aspects of the work and person of Christ. The term ίλαστήριον, the LXX. equivalent of "mercy seat," is in Romans iii. 25, applied to Christ, "whom God hath set forth to be a propitiation through faith in His blood." And this mercy seat aspect of Christ is regarded there as the very axis of reconciliation and harmony between those divine attributes expressed by the enactments, and those other divine attributes expressed by the offerings, viz., that God might be "just, and the justifier of him that believeth in Jesus."

Further, the mercy seat may, in accordance

with the above idea, be regarded as the meeting point of the superhuman intelligences, expressed by the Cherubim; of the visible creation, as summed up in the divine manhood; and of the manifestation of the Supreme, as mystically present on the Shechinah cloud between the Cherubim. Thus, then, we should have the idea of Christ's divine humanity in the tables; next the advancing idea of Christ's glorified humanity in the tables within the ark; and this, with its "covering," enshrined within the veil of the invisible world, and serving as a meeting point and centre of union and communion between God and His creatures, through the preliminary condition of sacrifice.

It is laid down for us that the act of the high priest entering once a year with the blood, and sprinkling it on, or rather, as the Jews hold, in front of the ark, is in itself a distinct representation of the one sacrifice, with the merits of which the Saviour has entered into the invisible heaven on our behalf. But it need not be necessarily supposed that the mysteries of the holy of holies stop short at expressing how heaven is opened. They may further typify the results of its being opened, and figure the policy which in the New Testament (Eph. i.) is described to be, "that in the fulness of times He might gather together in one all things in Christ, both which are in heaven and which are on earth." Nor would it detract from the typical propriety of this that Christ should also, in another relation, be described typically as once a year an offerer within the same place. Such combinations are not uncommon; indeed, it is generally allowed that he is in some senses victim, priest, and altar, and in the very transaction just referred to he is both the victim offered, the scape-goat released, and also the high priest sprinkling the blood. It may then well be that he is further figured as the eternal station of placability, in which the whole transaction completes itself, and is carried out to its fullest end.

There is little or nothing, perhaps, in such a view which we should regard with hesitation. Lightfoot, in treating on the contents of the inner sanctuary, well says: "Hanc partem benè attende et plenè videbis Christum."* Indeed, if we admit the altar at the door to be a direct type of Christ in part of his ministry, an admission which is general, it would seem unreasonable to deny that the ark, law, mercy seat, and cherubim in the most sacred centre of the shrine, have no corresponding direct reference to Christ. In concluding, then, we may adopt in part the sentiment of a writer of the beginning of the last century.† Solomon making all things new, made no new ark; for though ordinances and administrations may change, there can be no new Christ. As there is one God so there is one Christ, the same yesterday, to-day, and for ever. As the ark led Israel, so Christ leads us; as the ark defeated Dagon, so Christ defeats Satan for us; as Eli died of grief when the ark was taken, and the Bethshemites rejoiced exceedingly when they saw it returned, so Christ present is our joy—Christ absent our distress and decline. Like Christ, and because like Christ, the ark is the throne of grace (Heb. iv.), the manifestation of glory (Ezek. i. 9, 10.)

---

* Lightfoot in Exod. xxxvii.   † Mather.

and the speaking point of God. The mercy seat expresses Christ's passive submission and satisfaction (Rom. iii. 25; 1 John, 2-3). The law his active obedience—" Thy law is within my heart" (Ps. xl. 8). The Cherubim on the ark minister to him (Ezek. i; Is. vi. 2), and look towards the mysteries of the gospel (1 Pet. i. 12) held forth by the Church (Eph. iii. 10). See, then, the fulness of supply that is in Christ Jesus. Two things an enlightened conscience calls for—I cannot keep the law, and yet I want a perfect legal righteousness to appear before God in. Therefore Christ hath done it. Here is the law kept in the ark—" He hath fulfilled all righteousness." Again, I want a propitiation for sins committed. Therefore a mercy seat is upon the ark, for Christ hath not only kept the law himself but satisfied for our breakings of it.

CHAPTER XI.

THE tabernacle was to be the dwelling place of the Lord among His people. The divine presence, so far as specially localised, was to be within its veil, resting unseen in the most holy place. In the second sanctuary alone, outside this veil, worship was to be constantly carried on by the priests of the dispensation. The whole idea and manner of this arrangement was to be invaluable to Israel. By its donations and withholdings, its expressions and suggestions alike, it would give to their religion all the vivid impress of reality, which heathenism had aimed at producing, while it would at the same time depreciate, and withdraw the false and dangerous imagery by which heathenism had worked for its purpose. It would thus gain for times previous to the outpouring of the Holy Spirit, distinct objective expressions on these vital points of God's presence and providence, unseen, intangible, and yet fully real; and in doing so, instead of compromising the spirituality of later religion it would actually prepare for it.

While the fact of a God so really, directly, and continuously present, was a gift to believers in advance even of the pretensions of idolatrous systems, and while the very mystery of the presence was a perpetual disparagement of idolatrous methods, one thing alone would be wanting to make the tabernacle eminently missionary to communities beyond the tribes, viz., that the claims of its God should be substantiated and emphasised by works of power, so as to do away with any suspicion or charge that the invisible was but the unreal by another name, and so as to establish the divinity presiding over this new system as an actual force in affairs. This concession appears so useful, nay, so essentially requisite, for the purpose of setting and keeping the machinery of the plan in motion, that at once we incline to say, if allowable under any circumstances, then, most certainly, at this special point a series of marvels seems allowable and imperatively called for, as a necessary link in the chain of providences, by which the world

would have to be won at once back and
onward; and, instead of appearing gratuitous
or superfluous, such a series may well be
regarded as a fit and economical expenditure
of force.

All this, however, is a subject of proof elsewhere. It is referred to here merely to solicit
tolerance in any questioning mind, on behalf
of the august and beneficial truth of a substantial divine presence resident in the Hebrew
Shrine. Here it may be sufficient to say this:
if an outer revelation of God be, as we have
seen, a necessity for mankind, then such revelation must at any rate have two qualities—
first, it must be suitable to the men who
receive it; secondly, it must be suitable to the
God who gives it, that is, it must first be consistent with the antecedents, actual condition,
and coming prospects of the people; and,
secondly, it must accord with the principles of
the divine plan, promote the divine work, and
agree with the divine character. If we can
show this in the Hebrew system, we show
enough: for after all, when men object to the
marvellous among that people, do they not in

fact, by their very objection, prove the marvellous to be right? For what is in reality their meaning but this—that it appears fit to them God should act in a way they expect and are prepared to receive as appropriate. And is not that just the very thing He in fact did among the Hebrews whose expectations He fulfilled, and so was received by them? In the general principle there is no disagreement between the parties. God has, indeed, done just what the objector said should be done. There is only a disagreement in the application of the principle: the objector requiring that all infant and early ages of the world should be treated in the way quite appropriate to his own most refined age, and quite inappropriate to them, which would be unreasonable and also inoperative.

God, we may venture to think, will have sufficiently conciliated the mind of later times, when He exhibits within His ancient plans, fitted for the then present an admirable internal order of premonitions fitted to exercise the utmost ingenuity of ourselves, and to satisfy any reasonable questionings of ours by making it clearly seen, now, how He has been "declaring the end from the beginning, and from ancient times, the things that are not done." For, indeed, proofs of this sort, when multiplied and linked in together, to the immense extent we find in Scripture, coming up, joining and interlacing incessantly in all sorts of ways, are quite as mentally wonderful in our time as the physical wonder was in theirs, and as fitted for our state as that was for them.

In short the Bible is itself the master miracle. As such, like other miracles, it has been incessantly but in vain attacked; as such it is a conclusively evidencing witness on the revelations of God. Whatever one may argue of particular marvels there stands the whole Book itself an undoubted reality, and in some way or other to be accounted for by our age. One may object, as has been done so often, that miracles are not in accordance with what one sees of natural order in the world around; but, assuming this the case, and assuming it conclusive if it be the case, (neither of which concessions, however, could in reality be made), still we have before us the Bible itself. Where can another work be shown constructed under the same difficult conditions; representing different ages; flowing through different minds, mouths, and pens; taking different points of view; treating different affairs; recording different processes, and yet in all its parts speaking by many expressions the same things, and working always effectually towards one result, and in accordance with one set of principles, and these principles, too, but very partially embraced by its actors, and the full finalities of its plan in a great measure, if not altogether, hid away from them?

The Book itself, we say, is the first miracle to be encountered by our time, because the one especially addressed to it. Before dealing with the fancied difficulties of others we must dispose of our own; before coming to the particular objection on the wonders for an infant age, which wonders such an age we know would insist on having, we must answer this other wonder intended for ourselves, viz., the general construction, continuance, and power of the Bible. Until that is reasonably, fully, and philosophically done, and with allowance of the widest issues, it is premature to cavil at special particulars. Until it is done the orthodox believer may, on the fair habits of controversy, claim that the narrative shall be taken in its integrity as it stands, and serve, as it has always hitherto done, with such immense advantages as the basis of morals, faith, and hope.

We come then, again, to the tabernacle of the Hebrews, where the Lord unseen resides in wonders and in regarding it, since the things enacted among the tribes were not for themselves only, but for a future and wider Israel as well, their sanctuary we may expect will have meanings not only for them but also for all the Church.

This general completeness and comprehensiveness of the design begins perhaps to find expression in the very proportions of the structure where we find multiples of three repeatedly arranged in cubes; the marked figures, "three" and "four," bringing in the "seven" expressive of mystical completeness. The inner unseen sanctuary, it is allowed, ex-

presses the sacred realities of the invisible
heaven, where none ever enters save the
typical high priest alone, and that, in such
completed period, but once for all.

The outer sanctuary, where the priests
stand daily ministering, expresses therefore by
proportionate relation the Church visible and
conditioned in time. To this from the inner
sanctuary, where divine presence, processes,
and results reside in mystery, may it not well
be that there pass out, in figure as in fact,
through the veil two effluences. The first of
these, because repeatedly the first placed in
the lists, will be the "pure table," with its
twelve loaves, representing the nationality of
Israel in its twelve tribes, and, again, more
widely representing renewed society at large in
its civil aspects; and these twelve arranged in
two groups of six, even as borne by the high-
priest by their very names on his shoulders,
and so the whole of this society, shown as
presented, by means of the religious work in
hand, before the Lord, and constantly supported and maintained by Him in that attitude
and state; a renovation of the whole occurring

at each period of refreshment in the Sabbath
rest, and then a special incense of praise going
up and in, from earth to heaven, the whole an
offering " most holy," and rendered so through
the agency of the one high priest, by whom it
gains sanctification, and acceptance from within
the veil.

Secondly, and over against the shew bread on
the other or south side of the accessible tabernacle, stands the lamp with seven branches; a
number, may be, representing, first, Israel in
its religious development, and then more fully
the Church at large, the light of the world by
the Spirit of Christ which is in it; and these
branches lighted and trimmed, and supplied
with oil, accepted and sanctified, and all
this still carried on by the high priest, who
is typical of Christ, even as before the shew
bread was accepted and ordered, and offered
by him. The whole thus expressing Christ,
acting in the outer visible sphere, ordering
and sustaining and blessing incessantly from
the heaven unseen, both civil society and
religious life, and imparting to them the
gifts of the two tables; that is, the realisa-

tions of religious and social duties, which are
both written and for ever kept within his
own self, and which from him are to pass out
by the Spirit into his two-fold organisation;
so that by the keeping his sayings, his and his
Father's presence is attained, and men without
are drawn into the unity within, and religion
and life, even outside. the veil, are already
" most holy " unto the Lord.

As previously hinted, the incense altar does
not occur next in order of thought, but at this
point the theory, after giving significant directions for the construction of the tabernacle
itself, passes outside to that which now
becomes pressingly important, the altar of
burnt-offerings placed before its door.

At the very door of the sanctuary stood
the *one* sufficient four-square altar of all Israel,
the only place of atonement; the blood of
which was the means and occasion of entrance
within. It was stationed there by divine
appointment, and thus this great patriarchal
agency of worship, introducing and giving
occasion for the added developments of
Hebraism, expresses the continuous unity of

the general system, and shows that in its plan the substantial meanings of the past had to be gathered up as additions to the future, so that while on the one hand typical anticipations have prevented the evangelical from being altogether new, evangelical elements have prevented the old from becoming altogether obsolete.

But this altar thus placed by divine command showed more than this. While the ritual revealed from the mount at first left the great periodical festivals, as of more national significance, to their place in the " judgments," the sacrifice ordered in the actual primary revelation in the mount itself is the simplest, most primeval, and yet fullest expression of the rite—one lamb of the first year every morning, and one lamb of the first year every evening; " this shall be a continual burnt-offering throughout your generations, at the door of the tabernacle of the congregation, before the Lord," thus most emphatically collecting the whole idea from the offering of Abel to the copious imagery of the Book of Revelation, and placing it as an essential condition at the threshold of the new system.

And now it is that passing inwards, along the central line, the directions proceed from the altar of burnt-offerings at the door to the incense altar within the sanctuary, and placed in the very front, before the veil where the high priest was to offer, night and morning, "a perpetual incense before the Lord throughout your generations," thus expressing in symbol the prayers of the visible church, made acceptable after or in relation to the work of atonement on the outer altar, and through it become an eucharistic sacrifice, acceptable in the holiest within; a "glorifying and giving thanks to the Lord God for his great glory;" an "offering and presenting of the soul and body to be a reasonable, holy, and lively sacrifice unto Him in Christ," and a prayer that by the death of the lamb the believer and the whole Church might obtain remission of sin, and all other benefits of its typical death: an altar "most holy unto the Lord," to which answers flow back from within on to the twelve-fold shew bread and the seven-fold lamp.

Some consider that from this the idea passes in to the mercy seat, within the veil, to find in that a third and final altar. It may be questioned, however, whether this be the real method of the Scripture. Its utterances seem to go the other way. Thus, in assigning their duty to the Kohathites, in Numbers iii. 31, it says, " And their charge shall be the ark, and the table, and the candlestick, and the altars, and the vessels of the sanctuary," &c., an enumeration which does not include the mercy seat among the altars.

In one sense it is true the ark and mercy seat may be regarded as an altar: that is, when regarded as representing the work, attributes, and position of Christ. But Christ is so far an altar as this, that in Him is complete the fulness of sacrificial values; he being, as already said, the final realisation of both offerer, priest, victim, and altar. If, then, ever it seems the ark and mercy seat can only be rightly regarded as an altar in the temporary relation, when the high priest enters within the veil, with the blood, on the one day of atonement, for then we shall have together the one sacrifice once offered, the one presenter of its merits, and the one place, condition, or station of acceptance, viz., that one typically perfect structure, within which alone dwells for ever the full law, written by the very hand of God, and on which rests for ever, while the angel orders keep guard around, the mysterious presence of the appeased and complacent Divinity.

At this point let us pause to look back. We have seen that happy law of Paradise, in which duty was merged in love, broken for the sake of self. From that time we have seen self usurping power, until the earth was filled with violence and bloodshed, and some mighty individual self subdued all others around under a tyranny. These others, selfish also, lost by degrees the power of looking up in love to the holy God, and fell into a state in which reflections of self's own passions and ideas served self for deity.

To bring the world back from social miseries thus aggravated by the miseries of false religion, God, moving on in His work, called forth a man unselfish enough to leave country and

kin, and all near prospects and ties, trusting
in an unseen Being, and in the promise
of an unknown future. Thus Abraham long
lived free, apart from the corrupted rulers
of this world, except when at intervals he
was shown as their superior. He lived consciously in the presence of the one God,
and he pleaded before Him the sacrifice
of the ancient rite. His descendants of the
third generation were led down to face the
greatest tyranny and most elaborated idolatry
of the age, and after many and long vicissitudes
they were brought out in great strength, the
nucleus of a nation, illustrious by a brilliant
success over tyrant and idol, under a leader,
Moses, who proclaimed Abraham's God as
their ruler and their sole worship.

This extraordinary revival, thus launched in
the world was at the outset secured by a
written charter of freedom and faith, viz., one
God for unselfish worship; one fraternity
of neighbours for unselfish offices of duty.
Capacities lying hid in the future, yet fit to be,
to some extent, set out at the time, were
expressed in it by such prophetic method as

was adapted for the day, and while the arrangements of the commonwealth may have hinted the prospects of society, the ritual of the tabernacle clearly seems to have marked the coming development of religion. In its inmost shrine resided the embodied law of unselfishness, forming the central point for men and angels, and over which the divine presence forfeited in paradise once more smiled. The powers of this inner law, which had come from heaven on the mount, and returned to heaven in the tabernacle ark, flowed forth from the shrine to sanctify the nation as a community and as a Church, by their virtue applied through divine grace, while the sacrifice, ever one from the earliest times, though increasing in expressiveness as the system expanded, being offered as the entrance of their worship, led the soul on through connecting prayer to the very presence of Jehovah.

In the midst of these mysteries was to move a single figure of extraordinary dignity and importance, the high priest; a personage sanctified and set apart in perpetuity; consecrated

by elaborate rites; the prime mover in every
ceremonial; the recipient, preparer and dispenser of the grace given, given back, and given
again in constant reflux, as expressed by
sacred oil, ointment, and incense; the sacrificer,
and the presenter in the holy and inmost places
of the merits of the sacrifice. The tenour of
the Scripture does not place him before us as
merely the head of a priestly caste or college,
but rather all priesthood is summed up in him,
and the work of his subordinates is but the
reduplication or detail of some of his functions.
It is as if the account were labouring to explain
to us that in the minutely cared for array of
varied mysteries, the movement of the whole
was entrusted to one, and to one alone, who
could pass from the altar of sacrifice, through
the altar of prayer, into the very secret recesses
hallowed by the divine presence.

Account for it as we may it is difficult to
conceive a more effective and admirable representation of " the great high-priest that is
passed into the heavens, Jesus the Son of
God," than is afforded by this preliminary
official. His very garments are elaborately

cared for, and all parts of them lend themselves to carry on the symbolism of his office, expressing his sacrificial, prophetic, and governing functions, and showing in figure, by the ordering of their tribes in threes on the breastplate, how, in the heart of the "great high priest," are safely written the spiritual interests of his people. Showing, also, by the arrangement of their names, in two sixes, on the shoulder-pieces of the ephod, (the same order as in the shewbread,) how the government of their temporal interests is borne upon his shoulders. Besides this, still further emphasis is given to his status, by the elaborate and significant ritual of his consecration and purifications, which both impress with the idea of the inadequacy of the man himself, and of the greatness of the mysteries among which he is called to officiate.

To speak generally, this whole revelation of ritual is an adaptation of the first table in accordance with the religious wants of the time, and as it concludes with a renewal of the command to keep the Sabbath, we thus seem to have, in an incidental way, a corroboration of

the view that the fourth commandment is the
concluding one of the first table. On the
Sabbath, which is first marked as the expressive period of repose, and most fitly so, as it
recurs with most beneficent frequency, there is
to be rest; rest for all; rest in relation to the
divine rest; rest in the Lord, round his sanctuary and in emphatic reduplication of his
sacrifice. The very idea of it is so associated
with the holiest aspects of life, that the very
command to keep it with strict observance
sounds almost less like an injunction of duty
than a pledge of promise that the issue of the
plan should be a restoration from the world's
maladies, and a better return to the once
forfeited Eden.

It may be an assumption to say such a
system as this, braced up and compacted like
its own tabernacle, by an immense number of
minutely fitting parts, needed but to become
known to benefit the world, by competing
with its gross idolatries on the one hand, and
with its chimerical philosophies on the other.
But, at any rate, a most ingenious set of arrangements, a most happy combination of circum-

stances, or some cause or other, has, as a matter
of fact, secured for this religious system the
widest publicity among the most enlightened
nations, and it has in reality had among them,
in an amazing degree, the effects of checking
men's selfishness, and promoting their social
prosperity and religious elevation. From them
it has spread into other affiliated nations,
until the state of affairs begins to show it
not improbable that some day the system of
the Hebrews, with the religion of Jesus based
on it, will predominate over the whole world,
and the ancient prospect be fulfilled that the
kingdoms of the earth shall become the kingdom of the Lord and of his Christ.

Scepticism, no doubt, will always make
special efforts to discredit this part of Scripture, apparently so easy to attack, and yet
essential to the integrity of our system. But
this weakness is only apparent. The more we
walk round about it, and regard its bulwarks,
the more shall we find how, like the smooth
grass-grown slopes of a fortress, the Mosaic
covenant has strength within strength, and an
underlying system of complete defences. The

difficulties of doubt repeat themselves age after age, as do also the replies of belief. And, though both of them take forms of expression from the quality of the time, both in substance remain unchanged. The scepticism which has never prevailed against us we may be confident never will, and though always advancing as to a final victory, it will still, as of old, have to recede discomfited.

Such philosophy, indeed, can only offer us its own heroes instead of ours. But what can be said in comparison with our religion to authority like theirs, so transient and so soon discredited? Only what Origen said to Celsus, that while the teachers he would set up had given no instruction or laws which had proved useful to a single tribe, a whole nation scattered through the world, still gave obedience to Moses: that while the writings of his proposed teachers soon passed into neglect, the laws of Moses had stirred up many, even aliens to the manners of the Jews, to believe that, as the writings testify, the first who enacted these laws, and delivered them to Moses, was the Creator of the world. " For,"

added he, " it became the Creator of the
Universe, after laying down laws for its
government, to confer upon his words a power
which might subdue all men in every part of
the earth."

CHAPTER XII.

FAITH not merely leads to, but likewise results from, a changed estate. While it extends the prospect, and redirects the footsteps, it does so because insight is cleared and energy invigorated. It brings in a realisation of freedom, through conceptions and movements of freedom, but only because a germ of freedom has preceded all. In this power of faith the Hebrews, as Eusebius allows of them, were inferior to their ancestors. Instead of the open hills they had been in the straitness of Egypt. Instead of the altar to Jehovah they had been among the fanes, ritual and images of legendary gods, while the predominant personality of Pharoah had been stationed in front of all their outer activities.

The pure results of evangelical faith seem less attainable by persons so conditioned, and to secure reception by them of its deposits, it would appear imperatively needful to bring out a man for them into a prominence counter-

balancing the idea of Pharoah; to bring out a
cultus for them, competing in expressiveness
with what they had long had before them, and
to reveal the realities of heaven in some sort of
proportion to the pretentions of the familiar
shrines. All this had now actually been done,
and both the fact and the manner of its doing
furnish admirable testimonials to the divine
origin of that wisdom which has presided over
the transactions of Scripture.

In the midst, however, of the series of
supports there is suddenly found occurring a
stone of stumbling, and not unfitly, for without
a moral test how can moral action advance?
Without analogies of circumstance how can
the wider conditions of the future church be
foreshadowed? Prepared for, though it was,
by many assuring incidents, guarded by the
best arrangements possible, and presided over
by a divine apparition in the Mount, still,
notwithstanding all, the withdrawal and dis-
appearance of Moses for the complete periodic
space of forty days was no doubt in the nature
of a trial to Israel. It may have been necessary for his own establishment; it may have

been an indirect promotion through after humiliations for the people themselves; it may have been the only way of passing the divine mysteries into the human consciousness, and it may have been typically requisite as an expression of the larger dealings to come, but still a sort of trial it undoubtedly was, and under it the Hebrews failed.

Their transactions had been so far patently in the hands of the mediator,* and when he disappeared they probably thought him slain among the thunders, and lost for ever. Nor was such terror altogether unnatural in them, since in relapses, especially in early ones, men return all the way back to their old state. Danger was in those days usually associated with the divine, " Let us go to sacrifice to Jehovah our God," pleaded Moses to Pharaoh, "lest he fall upon us with pestilence or the sword." "Speak thou with us and we will hear," had said the people, "but let not God speak with us lest we die." And among the heathen this δεισιδαιμονία carried to excesses of superstition was in itself occasion of many

* Augustin, 'Quæst. super Exodum,' 149.

corruptions. What, then, should be done by Israel in the new emergency ? If the mediator himself was lost, who else could venture up to God ? God, therefore, must be brought down to them by the potent spell of the image, and localised by this familiar expedient in their midst.

The point at which any special appreciable expression of the divine person, qualities, or gifts occurs is the point of crisis in all religion. That the divine should come down to meet us at such a point seems essential, but the resulting risk is that man, not content to rise by godliness to the real station of meeting, may endeavour to draw down heavenly things still beyond this altogether to earth, and while retaining them in hostage for supposed spiritual benefits may continue himself in worldliness. Such has been the case, even in modern religion, and still more so in ancient. The Hebrew is here, as in so many other passages of his career, the typical man, and the events moving around him, the abiding admonition for all. The idolatry, into which he fell back, was an expression in the most poignant degree of this complete reversal of the conditions of the inner life. Its outer forms and corrupt cultus symbolised and illustrated it, and the creed, conduct, and society of its votaries carried it out.

Several subtle qualities in our nature and position seem to make inevitable this result, which experience has shown to be invariable, viz., that when men have brought down the idea and expression of God among them, by such forcible expedients, they will have also brought many evils and cares, and will fall into a state charged with recurring and increasing difficulties. It was in regard to these difficulties the Hebrews were to be seen labouring, subdued, and rescued, that through them the warning and rescue might be extended to all nations. And this was to be achieved by a prolonged experiment of extraordinary ingenuity. The plan was to preserve and invigorate the central system of sacrifice, so as to give advancing point, value and complexity to its meanings, which were by and by to culminate in the grandest crisis.

The plan was further to model life in such

a close organisation, and by such a strict rule, that each one of the incidents of depressed society, and idolatrous habit and superstition, should be in turn assailed and outlawed. It was to call forth a noble series of heroic incidents, which should enlist national enthusiasm and patriotic spirit on its side, and which should also contain within them the arranged resemblance to still higher personages and still wider events. It was to appeal to the strong impulses of interest on behalf of property and family guaranteed by it; most extraordinary of all, it was actually to take the very colours off the idolator's palette; to draw with them a true portraiture of the divine, so that at last this dangerous depravity was, like a drug in the physician's hand, to be forced into salutary combinations—we mean, that by a most sagacious arrangement of similarities and dissimilarities the law generally, and especially the legislation of the tabernacle and ritual, was to cull in the very field of Zoan a civilisation and worship which were to be the most powerful antidote to tyranny and idolatry, and the happiest introduction to the expanding life and religion of the better future.*

Such was to be the redemption, and like the meter of the rising Nile, the method fitly first indicates the lower state of man. The people in a mass come upon Aaron and demand an idol. His authority it seems they felt would be necessary to translate Jehovah into this baser presence. If so, his responsibility in yielding was increased. He gave way to them, and laboured in the work. They accepted the divinity of the image, identified it with their wonder-working patron, hitherto unseen, and Aaron proclaimed for it " a feast to the Lord." Burnt-offerings and peace-offerings were sacrificed, and then there was a sacrificial meal and, as idolatry ever needs, a passage of licence.

This was a quick turning aside out of the commanded way, a voluntary corruption ; and Aaron was its easy tool. Were his orders doubtful?   " Tarry for us until we come again." Did he question for Moses' safety? He had himself proofs on this, for he, his sons

* Maimonides' ' More Nevochim.'

and the elders of Israel had been in the mount;
had seen there the God of Israel, "and upon
the nobles of the children of Israel He laid
not his hand." Aaron afterwards admitted
his motive. He had seen the people to be set
upon mischief, and fearing them, as Pilate
feared the Jews, though unconvinced, he
yielded.

How honest the Scripture narrative! Josephus omits the circumstance altogether. Philo
refers to it, but suppresses the complicity of
Aaron. The Bible (accused of priestcraft)
exposes the high-priest. By its very colloca-
tion of the incidents which it records, a most
pressing indictment is framed. It shows us
God in the unseen sphere, solicitously arranging
a worship for men ; beautifully reducing into
typical miniature the glorious counsels of
redemption, and placing over the whole one
presiding figure alone; consecrating him by
long ritual elaboration, and appointing him to
stand between Himself and Israel. This one
figure is the high-priest. He it is who is to be
the agent of sacrifice ; the presenter of its
merits; the pleader of it in prayer, and the

NN

sole enterer within the veil. He is to order
the " bread of faces," and the sacred lamp ; to
apply the blood in the sanctuary ; to burn the
incense ; to use the ointment. And now
Moses will have to go down and see how this
man, just nominated for such honours, is at
the time engaged. Lately eating bread before
God, he is now partaker at an idol feast.
Depository of already revealed truth, he is
lending himself to a lie. Present custodian of
the commandments, he is the chief in breaking
them ; future custodian of the tabernacle, he is
now over the ritual of an image.

How emphatically does the sacred narrative
here at once give it to be known that this
earthly high-priest, so deficient in himself, can
but be the shadow of a mightier Mover unseen,
since even as it is about to set him in action,
it recites his incapacities and reproach. In
doing so it has this great effect—it the more
distinctly reserves to our great High-priest of
the Gospel those realities which the other was
so weak to embrace, and which even at the best
he could only apprehend partly, and enact
in a pageant. This very fall of Aaron, too,

before his investiture, writing as it does incompetency on the forehead of all earthly ministry, prepares us for declensions which, in every seeming absence of the Divine Personality, have passed upon His Church, and warns us to allow that whenever "holiness to the Lord" can be truly inscribed upon a priesthood, the whole and continuous gift of sufficiency must be from Him.

But the narrative is still further pointed. While the coming Aaronic priesthood is thus a failure below, a real mediation is conflicting successfully above. The progress of this mysterious struggle is set out with a wonderful refinement in relation to later developments, affording at once strong presumptions in its favour. The Lord announces to the mediator the fall, "Thy people have corrupted themselves." The word "thy" seems to show the divine wrath consciously in contact with the restraining power of an opposing advocate. And such, indeed, Moses was. On this very site he had been pressed, though unwilling, into the work, and had been told by Jehovah to go to Pharaoh, to bring the people out into a good land and a large. But now wrath would have itself let loose to cancel this. "Let me alone," it says to the mediator; "Do not plead thy right gained through my commission. Let me destroy them, and in thee will I fulfil my promise, and thou, in their stead, shalt become a great nation." Wrath in this is seeking a return to the ground of Noah—a clean recommencement, and so a putting back for generations of the work.

But not so the mediator. He will see not "my" but "thy" people. He will only see in such an issue the failure of the Exodus and the triumph of Egypt. He will not start as himself father of a new nation, but will go on the old line as a son of Abraham, and heir of the promise; so he calls on wrath to remember and fulfil the sacred oath to the patriarchs of a seed numerous as the stars and the land in possession for ever.

The triumph of this mediation, which retains in so severe a crisis a firm hold on the rock of Christ, as yet in a great measure beneath the historical surface, is complete, though its success seems, for reasons we can divine, not at the moment fully announced. This prospective Christianity has cast anchor within the veil. The only one free from complicity in the guilt of the people—the one for them, yet above them—has resisted the wrath, and let in the love, "and the Lord repented of the evil which he thought to do His people."

But a truly drawn mediator "is not a mediator of one." He should be able to reflect feeling, and take up action, for either side in turn. Coming back to the camp, Moses himself sees what God had before seen—the idolatrous fall of Israel. And so now is the turn for his anger also to wax hot. The covenant law is broken; he casts down and breaks the tables, its testimony. As far as in him is, he in this would seem to cancel Israel's covenant. As far as in him is, he next makes the people swallow the retribution of their sin; nor in this does he spare his own brother. Here wrath is moving in the mediator, as before in the Lord.

How admirably drawn is this picture in all its parts! We have the strict severity, and the yielding pity, in whose diversity the unity of divine love still manifests itself. We have the mediation in its turn reflecting and calling forth these divine phases. We have, in short, an exact anticipation of the attitude of Christ; an expression, even an explanation, of His work; a transaction in the mimetic heaven and earth, representing proportionately His mediation and dealings in the real heaven and earth. The whole an illustrious proof that the documents which thus both expressed and kept concealed this grand transaction until the fulness of time, contain indeed the counsel of God in a mystery.

In vain does the ingenuity of respectful criticism seek to unwind integument after integument, and to show us that the vitality it affects to reverence is but a mummy of the past. The incessant interlacing of the old and the new in Scripture, the harmonious attachments with which the Law and Gospel perpetually fit in together, present to us mentally that conclusiveness of evidence which the two parts of an indenture brought together and found to fit in mechanism and in construction produce to us in common affairs.

But to return. The strong action of Moses

among a people set on mischief, now brings on
a threatening of revolt. The prophet calls for
aid. Standing in the gate of the camp he
invites to him all who are on Jehovah's side.
The Levi tribe comes out and ranges itself for
the Lord. Its consecration is at this its passing
over from the traditional to the distinctive
revelation. It arms; and since every man in
the camp has sinned against his brethren by
idolatry, Levi, now representative agent against
sin, passing from gate to gate, is to smite in
judgment all who stand to oppose them ; thus,
at the first presenting an exact analogue of the
incidence of judgment in later revelation. In
the conflict three thousand rebels are slain,
and the idolatrous reaction is defeated.

On the next day deep dejection prevails,
and the prophet, still in accord with succeeding phases of his cause, after again
declaring to the people the greatness of their
sin, returning to the side of pity and love, goes
up to see if peradventure he may be able to
make atonement for them.

Their spiritual disorder was indeed great.
They had bent (prostrated themselves) before

an image, but they were stiffnecked before the Lord. They preferred old habit to new rule; Egyptian licence to patriarchal purity; feeble superstition to fresh evidence of power; self-indulgence to gratitude, and expediency to their solemn pledge. This showed their constitution carnal, cold, and worn, and their cure, difficult, if possible. Their advocate, therefore, in his pleadings, had already at once taken the case beyond them into another range. God's honour among the nations was not to be jeopardised, though His chosen were unworthy; God's covenant with Abraham should still hold, though Abraham's descendants had broken theirs. Nothing could be more just than this, the attributes of God being truly regarded, and it prevailed. In doing so it places before us in brief the whole problem of Judaism, and the key to its subsequent phases, viz., God working for His name's sake, and for His covenant's sake, and so sparing and yet visiting; exactly in short, by accepting the plea, accepting the position which finds expression in chapters xx., 5-6, and xxxiv., 6-7, " merciful and gracious, long-suffering, and abundant in goodness," and yet "that will by no means clear the guilty;" thus furnishing one more among innumerable instances of the full and intimate consistency essentially woven into the texture of the whole narrative.

It would be good for the training of the mediator himself that there should not be an immediate declaration of the effect of his great plea for mercy to the weak for the sake of one stronger, prior, above and yet belonging to them. It would be good he should not surely know the mercy till he could well measure the mercy, and so only after his sight of sin, his own anger, punishing and forgiveness of it, was he to come up again, and see and estimate the frame of the Divine counsel so sublime in pity and pardon. It would be good also, if the whole transaction was to have its effect as expressing the general idea and course of mediation, that the full results should not be anticipated, but that the human agent should pass uncertified through the various stages, and thus be enabled to reflect more fully the phases of the process. For thus man's discoveries become God's promulgations,

and human justice and mercy are a comment
as well as a fulfilment of the Divine. They
are thus, also, a vindication of it; for the
breaking of the tables, the accusation against
Aaron as tempter, the enforced drinking of
water with idol dust, show Moses himself of
the same mind as God.

The leader now returns, and once again before
the Lord pleads in the mount for Israel—now
" this " people instead of " thy " people. " For-
give, and if not let my hopes cease as well." Such
is his spirit, true in affection even as Paul's
" I could wish that myself were accursed from
Christ for my brethren," but ineffectual to
save as all mere human effort must be. Atonement is reached towards, but not reached; and,
indeed, the impossibility of its being so reached
is thus indirectly announced, and the way for
the future mediator of a better covenant kept
open. Whosoever hath sinned he it is, and he
alone, who shall be blotted out of God's book.
Moses is to go and lead the people to the
place spoken of, and " mine angel shall go
before thee." Thus there is long-suffering,
and yet in the day of visitation their sin shall

be visited on them. The Lord's providences will move on in judgment and in mercy combined. His punishment will be upon the guilty persons, while the pardoned people shall be saved.* The Church shall endure though its members fail; the body shall be preserved though its particles waste out. "Thus the Lord plagued the people because they made the calf which Aaron made."

Further, God said they were to go to the land promised by His oath to the fathers; that He would send an angel before them, and drive out the sinful nations, whose iniquity was full, and whose day of visitation had now nearly come; but that He would not go up in the midst of them, lest, as they were so obstinate against Him, His wrath breaking forth, He should consume them in the way. So then His very withdrawals are in mercy, and the limit of His graciousness is not in Him but in ourselves.

Further still; as they had been prepared by cleansings for hearing and accepting the law, so now by stripping off their ornaments

---

* Ezek. xiv. 13. Cyprian, de Lapsis, 19.

of Egypt were they to prepare for hearing and submitting to the sentence on breaking the law. In their midst it was to be decided whether in their midst the all-righteous Jehovah could go up without causing their destruction; whether by ready humiliation and softening to penitence they could hope to survive in that presence. The rest of their jewels, not already gone in the calf, were now discarded for good, and the spoilers of Egypt seem here to abjure their spoil.

We may observe how the Law had already achieved an immense result. It had succeeded in placing Israel in its real position. It had revealed to them the sinfulness of man's heart before Jehovah, and had brought them in penitent humiliation to His footstool, thus in reality giving them "greater riches than the treasures of Egypt." The whole work it was to do throughout time for mankind we here see it immediately setting in motion, leading them at once by its since well-worn steps to the meeting point with Christ. Moses, himself led along in action to express this, now takes a special tent, "and pitches it without the camp, afar off from the camp," and "every one which sought the Lord went out" unto this tent without the camp (Hebrews xiii. 13). Thus, in the hour of their deep prostration, Jehovah was no longer before them as when a warrior host, or above them as when a covenanting body, but more graciously still among them as His poor fallen tolerated people, and accessible to all, even as each might will to seek, thus occupying the gospel position in the gospel hour.

But in these partial proceedings there was evidently more to come. If the covenant Moses pleaded was a power to save, it might also be a power to restore. With such a mediator a more intimate effort at mediation was therefore sure to ensue. Moses goes out to the tent of meeting; the people in reverence regard his approach to it; the cloud of the Divine presence descends on his entry into it; while the people, each in the door of his tent, worship at this Divine recognition of their leader and his work.

The circumstance is evidently one of central meaning. On one side is Sinai, representing heaven, on the other side the camp, representing the people of God. According to later religious development, the action should pass at this point into the hands of one man. One man we here accordingly find at work. A single tent is placed between the two spheres, and there one advocate on behalf of the people communicates with the Lord, who descends especially to meet him. This one, if we are led in our anticipations by New Testament form, should be one especially dear, and so we here find him. He is spoken to as no other is, face to face, as a man would speak to his friend. He is not regarded only as included in the patriarchs; he is looked on in his individuality as well, and has himself (παρὰ πάντας, LXX.) found grace in God's sight.

This is a peculiarity distinct from ordinary course of Scripture, that one should be both within the originally declared covenant, and also above it, and yet so exact is the balance of the New and Old Testaments that this very peculiarity keeps up the resemblance of Moses to Christ. For his sake things are done, and to him revelations are made, not as to other prophets, but in intimate way of confidence. In accordance also with the mission of our Lord he has a special charge—" Thou sayest unto me, Bring up this people." They are to be taken from the lower to the higher country; from Egypt to Canaan, as in the fuller work, from earth to heaven.

But as our blessed Lord, having it for His mission to bring up the people of God, and for that end tabernacling among us, was to win for us the perpetual presence of the Holy Ghost, so here we are to see the typical mediator, while engaging in his typical salvation, full.of anxiety on this essential question of the inner presence and help, which is to preside in and advance the outer work. Moses pleads the true mediatorial plea in the true spirit. He has a charge to bring up the people, but " Thou hast not let me know whom Thou wilt send with me." He now pleads by his past acceptance for a revelation on this, that knowing Jehovah's way he may know Him, and so gain further acceptance for the tribes—for, adds he, " consider that this nation is Thy people." Here we almost seem

to have old Israel again before us, wrestling
for His blessing. It is granted to the mediator.
"My presence shall go with thee, and I will
give thee rest;" that is, "the land of rest."
But the concession thus conditioned to himself
with exact typical propriety, he, with the
same propriety, at once passes on to the
Church. "If thy presence go not, carry us not
up hence. For wherein shall it be known
here that I and Thy people have found grace
in Thy sight? Is it not in that Thou goest
with us?"

Moses had seen more of God than any man;
more, therefore, than any he would see still
more of Him. He has just seen His grace.
"I beseech Thee," he therefore adds, "show
me Thy glory." He is answered, that man
cannot see this in its splendours, but shall in
the procession of its workings. So Moses is
to go up alone into the mount, bearing two
other tablets of stone. And here God again
descends in the cloud, stands with him and
proclaims the name and attributes of Jehovah.
In this mount, at the prophet's first call, had
been made known to him God's completeness

in Himself; now is revealed to him there God's completeness for His people; mercy, grace, long-suffering, abundant goodness and truth, riches of forgiveness, and equity of retribution.

When they had been in straits of bondage, the prospect set before them in Exodus iii. 8 was that the Lord would "bring them up out of that land unto a good land and a large." When they had stood before the holy mount to receive a nationality and a religion, then the promise was in Exodus xix. 6, that they were to be a kingdom of priests and a holy nation. Now that they had fallen, and the Levi or priestly tribe had executed among them the typical judgment of the Lord, who "will by no means clear the guilty,"—now it was here made known that a terrible thing was to be done also among the nations by their agency as the priestly nation.

An order is given to make no treaties nor alliances with the land they go to, but to destroy its idols, to make none themselves, and to keep their own safe and significant solemnities strictly.

These solemnities are now recited. First is named the passover, with an emphasis on the blood of its sacrificial lamb, without leaven; and with this rite is associated the consequent rule of the first-born, who are by it the redeemed possession of the Lord. This great primary rite, now that their sinfulness has been revealed by the law, finds its full place, and is eminently expressive as a representation of the gospel sacrifice by which the Church of the first-born is redeemed. After the turning mark of the Sabbath comes, secondly, the Feast of Weeks or Pentecost, so generally believed a type of the descent of the Holy Spirit on the Christian Church, and associated with a characteristic offering of the first fruits of the produce of the commenced work and fruitfulness of the year. Thirdly comes the complementary feast of Ingathering or Tabernacles, when all the divine gifts of the completed harvest are garnered. This festival is accompanied by a rule supposed to be aimed against opinions and customs which attributed fertility and success to other agencies and powers, and not to God's provi-

dential mercy and covenanted promise; a promise which ascends in meanings from Noah to
Abraham, and thence on through Moses to
Him in whom all the promises of God are
yea and amen; in whom the fulness of the
spiritual harvest shall at length find completion in the ingathering of the last day, when
"the Lord alone shall be exalted" and "the
idols utterly abolished."

A second forty days had now been passed
in the mount.   Advancing developments of
gracious condescension and growth of the
revelation as regards the central personality
and work of the mediator have marked its
course.   Moses now descends with the recovered Law—renewed because man's fall
required it afresh; the same because the
divine word cannot change.   As he came
down from this residence with God, which
had been emancipated from the common conditions of human life, and which had endured
for a time representing in type a completed
cycle or perpetuity, there was seen reflected
in his face the glory of the presence in which
he had dwelt, even as in the fulfilments of the

appointed time men might behold "in the face of Jesus Christ" "the glory as of the only begotten of the Father, full of grace and truth."

The people were now assembled by their leader for the building of the tabernacle. Though their labour was to be for the Lord, their work was prefaced by a special injunction not to break the Lord's Sabbath; for obedience is better not only than sacrifice, but than all voluntary offerings, since God, in giving us a rule, has given more than we can ever give him. The "willing of heart" brought their offerings, the "wise of heart" gave their labour, until there was "more than enough for the service of the work."

The tabernacle was at length finished and the people blessed. It was reared and all things placed therein, Moses himself first arranging them. He it was who in person "set the bread in order," "lighted the lamps before the Lord," "burnt sweet incense on the golden altar," "offered the burnt offering and meat offering on the altar of burnt offering, "washed his hands and his feet at the laver."

"So Moses finished the work." And his first performance of so many ministerial acts prior to the consecration of Aaron shows that while the things of the Sanctuary are temporarily committed to priestly agency, representative for the time of the ultimate ministration within, yet that the mediator of the covenant is the essential priestly power and the full communicator with heaven. Thus the representative in the old dispensation in assigning over still reserves the rights of his principle in the new, and Moses is here, as ever, found preparing for Christ. "Then a cloud covered the tent of the congregation, and the glory of the Lord filled the tabernacle" in proof of divine acceptance, favour, and presence.

The wonders of the Scripture, like those of Nature, may well be for us practically inexhaustible. There are hardly any depths of meaning to which reverent research, carefully securing its steps, may not in either field be led, and as it advances such research may still ever be finding itself but at the brink of new and deeper discoveries. Here, in the minutely careful setting forth of the mediatorial pleadings of Moses, it is, as repeatedly put, highly possible that we may have before us a grand suggestion of the movement of the Redeemer along universal history. Thus the very first inducements—God's honour and the triumph of His plan—would be cogent motives from the beginning of man's course. The covenant, not with the parties concerned, but with another, their mediator and chief, and the patience asked for, not on their but on his account—the pardon granted them for this other's acceptance — take us back to the beginning of all things, the eternal covenant before the world began, and Adam saved through Jesus.

In all these things mystery lies within mystery, and each part, while in one aspect a step in a series, seems in another a complete germinal compendium of the whole work. But in the whole, as in all parts of it, Jesus Christ is still to be found. He is impressed on the progressive action. He animates each detail of the mechanism. He is at once the history and its actors; the ritual, the priest, and the tabernacle. The whole machinery is a divine apparatus; the whole movement is a divine advance; through the crevices and textures of the humanity of this selected people; through all done with them and by them there shines out a divine compelling splendour of truth and grace veiled and unveiled, shaded away and yet refusing to be hid; and in the midst of all the flittings, dimness, and shifting outlines of the twilight time we get to apprehend that the Almighty Lord is come forth to conquer the world into peace and love, and to cause His will to be done in it in pure life and pure religion, even as it is done in heaven. As we meditate on all this, we may well adopt as our final expression the sentiment of the pious Bishop Hall—"God grant that the veil removed from the face of Moses may never be drawn over our heads!"

APPENDIX.

PAGE 16.

Law of Nature.—While on the one hand Hebrew
Law was gradually expanding, under a vast variety of
influences, some ordinary and others of a special and supernatural sort, towards the point at which its two tables
were suddenly to bloom forth into the Divine personality
of our Lord and the holy charities of His Gospel, on
the other hand the system, both civil and religious, in
the great Roman Empire which was becoming the accredited power to give and withhold consents on behalf of
humanity was, by a corresponding proportion of advance,
gradually making ready to become the recipient of the
divine revelation. The stringencies of the ancient
Roman ideal, which represented with an almost Jewish
pertinacity methods of law from which the vitalising
spirit had long departed, were gradually toned down by
the prætors. The theory of equity had arisen as an expression of an independent general rule. Men had begun
to imagine that there existed something superior to all
municipal institutions. This they called the 'Law of
Nature.' Thus jurisconsults and philosophers were
moving in the same direction, or rather the principles of

Q Q

philosophy were penetrating the methods of law. Cicero, although he admits that certain unworthy conduct was, through the depravation of their customary rule, not deemed base as to morality, and was tolerated by law, yet feels sure it was not sanctioned by the Law of Nature. For there is, he holds, a most widespread social relationship, an inner circle, which comprehends those who are of the same nationality; a closer still those who are of the same community; and he regrets that the law they then had was by no means a solid and exact representation of 'true right' and 'genuine justice.'

Thus, together with this fertile thought of one general law independent of and above civil arrangements, there was also growing up within the Roman Empire the idea of a corresponding moral association among men at large. Though Plato had already put this forth, it had been rather with a limitation to the Greek races. Here again Cicero advanced. 'Among those,' he says, 'who have a communion of law, there is also a communion of right. Now those who have these things in common are also to be held as being members of the same civitas, so that the whole world is to be considered as 'una civitas communis deorum atque hominum' (*De Leg.* i.7). In Seneca we find this sort of conclusion still gathering weight. He regards mankind as something which should be sacred to men. The whole visible sphere appears to him a vast moral unity. He looks upon all as members of one comprehensive body, and he adds, 'Natura nos cognatos edidit quum ex iisdem et in eâdem gigneret. Hæc nobis amorem dedit mutuum et sociabiles fecit' (*Epist.* 90). This whole method of thought was provisional, an effort to break through the narrow hardness and deficiency of current systems, and to reflect and reach towards the coming light.

In the meantime, from the Jewish side, truths of stupendous power were entering the Roman world. St. Paul had declared 'in the midst of Mars Hill,' that 'God that made the heavens dwelleth not in temples made with hands,' 'neither is worshipped with men's hands, as though He needed anything ;' that He 'hath made of one blood all nations of men for to dwell on all the face of the earth,' that 'we are the offspring of God,' and that therefore 'we ought not to think that the Godhead is like unto gold or silver or stone, graven by art and man's device.' To Rome itself he had written, 'Owe no man anything, but to love one another, for he that loveth another hath fulfilled the law ;' and again, 'Is He the God of the Jews only? Is He not also of the Gentiles? Yes, of the Gentiles also : seeing it is one God which shall justify the circumcision by faith and uncircumcision through faith' (Rom. iii. 29).

This Law of Nature, imagined as resident among the instincts of conscience, may well have derived its real suggestions of origin from the Hebrew Law, for that latter system was throwing out the very widest principles in its sacred documents, and professed them the announcements of a divine ruler of the widest power. Clement Alex. affirms of it that Plato took even his ground idea from Moses whom he describes as a 'living law' ($\nu\acute{o}\mu o\varsigma$ $\check{\epsilon}\mu\psi\nu\chi o\varsigma$), and whose whole system he regards as 'suited for the training of such as are capable of becoming good and noble men.' And he argues that those

who really obeyed it had already some beginnings of the
knowledge of Christ, while those who disbelieved it or
disobeyed its precepts had no inclination for Him, since
He, the Word, was the 'wisdom and power of God.'
The Scripture teachers, however, do not enter into the
matter as into an abstract or inferential system. With
them it is the simple effective promulgation of binding
decrees accompanied by fitting sanctions. The definition of Ulpian makes Nature the teacher. Theory is
left for others ; among these Grotius bases Natural
Law on the dictate of right reason. Some following him
have it as the 'ratio summa insita in Naturâ,' in which
they approach by implication nearer the view of the
text, since they at the same time regard all existence
to be one single moving comprehensive Nature. But,
as Bishop Atterbury observed, the difficulty of 'right
reason as the basis is, whose reason shall it be?' Others,
therefore, have fetched the basis of the Law of Nature
from the general consent of men : ' Jus commune omnium
nationum, eo quod ubique instinctu Naturæ, non Con-
stitutione aliquâ, habeatur.' But it is found that many
communities have points at variance with the common
decision of men, therefore Selden and Puffendorf reject
this test, and the appeal is next made to the common
sentiment of humanity (Puff. xii.). Vico, in concluding
his Philosophy of History, insists that all the early governments in the world were founded on the belief in a
Providence, and had religion for their entire form, and
for the sole basis of the State and family. He regards
religion as the rampart of peoples. If it be lost to them
there remain no longer means for them to live in society.

They lose the very formative potentiality without which they cannot exist. Far from there being truth in the notions of Bayle or the suggestion of Polybius in favour of philosophy as the final motive power, religion alone, he holds, can excite the people to do from sentiment virtuous actions. The respect of the wise for antiquity is, according to him, only an instinct leading on to respect the infinite wisdom of God, and the philosophy of history must necessarily bear with it the inclination for piety, since 'sans la religion il n'est point de véritable sagesse.'

We conclude then that the idea of a Law of Nature was an abstraction gradually thrown up by advancing society become conscious through various agencies of the existence among men of a system higher and wider than municipal law, and we regard the very existence of the idea as a proof and admission of the necessity for such higher law, and as a preparation for its reception under Christ. The Mosaic germs may, as insisted by the ancient apologists, have penetrated into Gentile soil, and given its first vitality to the idea of Natural Law, and this would be admirably illustrative of the continuous harmony of the Scripture work. But even if the opposite conclusion be chosen, and it be held that the idea of the Law of Nature was built up independently and apart from Hebrew suggestions, then what a testimony have we to the wonderful propriety of that system which, in the infancy of a small and historically insignificant State, struck out for the Hebrews a plan wider in its scope, nobler in its equities, more vigorous in its sanctions, than the best efforts of the maturest heathen philosophers, and which further, instead of losing like them the summit of its system among mists and clouds, could place on its highest presiding throne the august presence of a distinct and consistent Personal God.

PAGE 58.

On abuses of the Paternal Power.—In the ruder states of society, when sentiments of liberty and right were weak and easily suppressed, history shows there was a constant risk of the power of the more authoritative domestic relationships passing on into excess. It is easy to understand that the best precaution against this would be such a religion as, while it sanctioned and supported these authorities, would not, like so many heathen cults, coalesce with them in attempts to step beyond their right spheres. It was the special characteristic of the Hebrew system to aim at this ; and not only by its express enactments, but equally effectively by its very construction, to bring them into constant contact with a higher authority of the same sort as their own, and one standing to them in the same degree as they stood to others —a contact which would necessarily tend to keep them to their true functions. Thus, while the Lord gave, in the Pentateuch, the fullest sanction to the domestic power of parents and others in authority, He yet claimed that all Israel was His son, His first-born, and presided over it as Parent-Chief. M. Renan has put forth a notion that until Jesus the idea of God as a father was hardly, if at all, conceived. This, however, is by no means in accordance with general ancient literature, nor with the Old

Testament, which is full of the thought, and which stu-
diously and successfully brought the Father-God of
Abraham into the closest paternal proximity with the
people. Indeed its method of re-knitting the ideas of
the regal, the paternal, and the divine into one operative
power, in the Hebrew consciousness, was both invaluable to them and prolific for the future of the world, and
the effort to interpose a mere secular royalty as a new
headship over the tribes, which was attempted in the
days of Samuel, would both be a shock to conscience and
also an experiment obviously dangerous when liberal sentiment was undeveloped, and when royalty, unprotected
by later checks of limitation, would, in following the paternal outline, so easily decline into tyranny; and the success of this ill-omened scheme brought on, as we know,
the ruin of the country, by letting in all those evils
against which the original constitution had been framed.
At the commencement of modern society several moderating causes happily prevented a similar result. The
feudal system was effective to give a strong stimulus to
some of the better incidents of tribalism, promoting as it
did generous and loyal feelings among the masses, and
securing at the early period, before popular institutions
could arise, a powerful class of chiefs as a barrier against
the encroachments of the crown. (See Hallam.) But
we must venture to add, notwithstanding the tone of that
writer, that nothing served so much to secure modern
societies from the ruin of ancient nations as the existence
among them of the Christian Church. This, even in its
most depressed states, helped to restrain the royal and domestic authorities within limits, and secured society from

the convulsions which had been so disastrous to the ancient world, and from which not even the most politic and advanced nations of them could without religion secure themselves.

The Roman State may very properly serve for an illustration of the condition of things to which we refer, for as the material power of the world became collected under Roman sway, so the whole spirit of the world grew to be condensed and intensified in the Roman system. The corrective force to meet this was in motion in the legislation and polity of Moses, on its side also developed and intensified into the Gospel. It is not meant that the whole Roman polity was antichristian, for much of it may have been the reverse. At any rate much of it has been adopted into the jurisprudence of Christian communities, and forms the ground-plan on which a vast amount of European law and social organisation is raised. What is meant is that within it there were certain pervading principles and tendencies which, even after all the mitigations they had received as civilisation advanced, still were opposed, and essentially so, to those interests of moderate liberty and domesticity of affections which Christianity so greatly favours, which had been the original thought in government, and which, there seems reason to believe, will be its final issue.

The Roman family was not a natural but an artificial creation. The fiction of power (potestas, manus) was the idea which bound up its members into an unity. The natural circumstance of being wife, son, or relative did not make one a member of the family, but the legal fact of being wife, son, or relative under power. A family was an aggregation of individuals bound together by their subjection to the authority of one head or chief, who, as Ortolan puts it was alone 'sui juris,' and who was master of all the persons and all the property, ' corps and biens,' of all the rest. Every one who could be considered under this authority was a member of the family. Everyone who was removed from it by *diminutio capitis* even if a child or grandchild, was no longer of the family. Into this artificial association entrance was by artificial processes. The higher sort of marriage, even (*justæ nuptiæ*), did not pass a woman into it; she remained in her own family as matrona. It was the religious ceremony of confarreation or the fictitious sale of coemptio which introduced her into the new family ' under power,' and she became materfamilias. But though she had this title, nevertheless, with the object that the central 'power' might not be encroached on, her position in the family was but that of adopted daughter, under a ' dominus'; she was in a sense only but as sister to her own children (Gaius. Inst. I. iii. 3); and it was in this character, if at all, that she succeeded to her husband's property (*Ibid.* iii. 3). His death, however, did not return her to her own family ; she remained in his, still dependent, under a legal guardian chosen from among the agnates, or under a testamentary guardian named by him (*Ibid.* i. 148).

By the side of this aggravation of one part of family authority we have in the Roman system another—that of ' power ' over the children. This absorbed into the father both the person of the son himself, of his wife, and of his family, together with all the property acquired by them. In the domestic forum the father was the sole judge, and without appeal or ceremonial by the untempered law could decide all things, even to the life or death of his children. So Plutarch says of Brutus that he condemned his son, not as consul but as father, without judicial forms. But this right, it should be observed, was not considered by the Romans as flowing out from natural relationship and as an incident following on all marriage, but only as following on a civil incident—the 'justæ nuptiæ' of the civil law or on adoption by the civil law process. All these persons thus artificially chained together, however ramified their offshoots, had among themselves the quality of civil relationship, which was regarded by the Roman system as a higher tie than that of nature itself. Thus bound by ' agnatio ' they alone were considered as forming fractions of the compound social unit called ' family,' an aggregation of which civil 'families ' united by a common patronymic and common sacrifices and rites made up the political unit of the ' gens. ' Within this civil family (or family as regards private relations as distinguished from the gens or larger body of connected families for the purpose of public relations) there was a complete system of domestic life. Successions and guardianships were arranged among its members alone. It had special domestic religious rites and special public sacrifices which were peculiar to it ; and yet the entrance to and exclusion from its area depended on such artificial conditions that the nearest natural relationships might be estranged from it, and ignored. Indeed the natural relationship of blood was in the Roman system treated as a far lower idea, and even a son who by emancipation passed from paternal power and became 'sui juris,' passed out of the family, and was reduced to the rank of a cognate (Gaius i. 132). So that for natural affection to get itself recognised it was necessary for it to put on the civil mask, and to speak in official costume (Vico).

The same artificial spirit had extended among them to property. The 'res mancipi,' that is, lands, houses, slaves, and cattle, could only be acquired by a State process, and only possessed by Roman citizens, though the 'res nec mancipi,' comprising all the various objects unimportant at the time when legal ideas took their form, but to which advancing civilisation had given enhanced value, could change ownership merely by delivery. Whatever price had been paid, whatever moral equity existed, unless the forms had been complied with, property of the higher class could not pass, and until prescriptive possession (usucapio) had come in to cure the vice, they might be resumed by the vendor in spite of all moral claim. And even this prescription would only help a Roman citizen ; all others must suffer without remedy.

This slavery to form and laxity of moral restraint extended beyond the family and property into the region of contract. Here, again, it was not feeling, conscience, and the idea of just and unjust which bound men, but the mere verbal form. The rule of the twelve tables was 'uti lingua nuncupassit ità jus esto,' and so whatever was outside the set words was held not to have been promised. Implied warranties were unrecognised, and the materialism of the system was powerless before combinations of fraud. This whole original plan of the 'Jus Quiritium,' as it was called by its older title, or 'jus civitatis' by its modern synonym, was essentially hard and tyrannical. The more so as it perpetuated externally patriarchal ideas whose successful working had been due to the cordial spirit which animated them—a spirit banished or confined under the Romans, and deprived of those salutary impressions on religious duties and on responsibility to a present personal Father-God which had so long vitalised the early laws of the Hebrews.

We repeat, then, that the Hebrew development, moving parallel with the civilisations of antiquity, was their effectual corrective. With God revealed as the head of its society, the parental was by it restored and restrained to its true functions, and this essential community was bound together by an improved feudalism in permanent cohesion. Though a rude shock had been received by it on the foundation of a secular monarchy, the balance of its action was in a measure restored through the developments of the prophetic under Samuel. And the whole body of the Hebrew state gradually moulding itself into shape, recovered from its aberration against the idea of divine unity, by its contact with Persia; gathered fuel for intenser patriotism in its struggles with the West, until, at last, permeated and fully vitalised by the splendours of Christ, the chosen Israel took a further flight, transforming the theocratic of Josephus into the more purely paternal of the Gospel, and shaking off the hedge of the Law, in favour of a full morality applied in the forum of the conscience. Thus, by the chosen people, the Divine Wisdom rescuing and giving the widest expansion to the pure family system, secured principles of perennial vigour, by which societies, renewing themselves, escape the bondage of the ancient world, and, in the individual, conscience is educated for Christ.

PAGE 114.

On the Historical Estimation of Moses.—A profound consistency pervades the Scriptures in their reference to this prominent figure. There is hardly a passage in either Testament which, even in appearance, diverges from strict historical keeping with the first central delineation, and the few which seem to do so are, in reality, deeper consistencies. It is extremely observable how the New Testament shows Him very firmly seated in the public reverence, and wound in with the fabric of national life, and how, though the whole movement of nationality takes him as its mainspring, in the Old Testament, yet a strict forbearance of statement constantly surrounds Moses in both cases. Notwithstanding temptations to transgress, succeeding scribes never seem to lose the sentiment of harmony with the original Bible theory, but advance along with it unerringly, in mixed modesty and boldness. In periods where Moses is made to stand out as the essential factor, he is still never allowed to encroach beyond his ground, as, for instance, on to the position of the father, Abraham. Beneath the national organiser there is still ever seen lying the deep immoveable foundation of that first patriarchal rock of faith and covenant promise. Yet, on the other hand, when the institutional, the didactic, and, perhaps, the mediatorial are in the field of vision, there a comparison is unhesitatingly

permitted, even with the 'prophet like unto me,' the
sacred Messiah Himself. When, again, the question of lea-
dership is uppermost, then Moses comes down in the narrative to group with Joshua, his minister, as in Josh. i., 5
and 17. A passage also occurs in which he is brought
into contact and parallelism with Samuel: 'Then said the
Lord unto me, though Moses and Samuel stood before me,
yet my mind could not be toward this people.' Jer. xv. 1;
and this grouping also is in full propriety, for the offence
of the people is there the point in issue, and this was, at
the time, a hardening of themselves in law-breaking, being
encouraged thereto by false prophecies of immunity from
the lips of lying prophets. Here, therefore, these two
would be the fit representatives to speak and plead—Moses
the recognised organiser of the legislative and admin-
istrative; Samuel the systematiser and trainer of the
prophetic. (Acts xiii. 29, 'until Samuel the prophet.')
So in Luke xvi. 29-31—the parable of Dives and
Lazarus—this same natural and accepted method of
division comes out: 'They have Moses and the prophets; Let them hear them,' i.e., the law and the prophets—Moses standing as representative for the Divine
Will in its original enactment, the prophets for the
same Will in its moral applications and extensions, as
distinguished from the technical administration of the
Scribes. So, again, in Luke xxiv. 27, our Lord 'beginning at Moses and all the prophets, expounded unto
them in all the Scriptures the things concerning Himself,' i.e., going through the two fields, the law and the
prophets. And in the former of these two passages
it is observable that the words are put in the mouth

of Abraham, whose position there is thus, by implication, the one of first eminence, far beyond all others.
The Old Testament canon ends in Mal. iv., 4 and 5,
by another arrangement bringing together Moses and
Elias:—4 'Remember ye the law of Moses my servant,
which I commanded unto him in Horeb for all Israel
with the statutes and judgments.' 5 'Behold I will send
you Elijah the prophet before the coming of the great
and dreadful day of the Lord.' Here law still contents
itself with the same representative, but prophecy passes
to a new figure to find expression, since it is going on
from the didactic to the more minatory phase. These
two great personages, here connected in the prospect of
the people, are grouped together in inner relationship by
the mystery which surrounds their passage out of life, by
the previous and, perhaps, preparatory mysteries of their
wonderful fasting, and by the vouchsafed vision of the
presence of God.

From these data it is therefore by a just transition that
we arrive at Matt. xvii. 3, where, at the transfiguration
of Jesus, 'behold there appeared unto them Moses and
Elias talking with Him.' The words of S. Luke, ἔλεγον
τὴν ἔξοδον αὐτοῦ (ch. ix. 31), suggest Moses; as the expression in Acts i. 2, ἀνελήμφθη corresponds with the
Septuagint of 2 Kings ii. 11. καὶ ἀνελήφθη Ἡλιού.

We are not required to suppose that the Scripture
contains all that was known of Moses. There is obviously in the early writings considerable reticence. While
the whole detail of his mission is copiously set out, a veil
is drawn over many of his personal antecedents, though
these could hardly have failed both to be interesting and,

to some extent, known to the nation. And it is this very economy which, in its admirably proportioned disclosures and concealments, will always, in itself, gratify and convince the more judicious and devout. The people had undoubtedly certain details treasured up among them, concerning their great prophet. A few touches of these we find accepted into the Scripture itself at a late period, as those contributed by Stephen in his defence, in Acts vii., and those in the Epistle to the Hebrews, as ch. xi., but they leave the idea and position of the character unchanged. In the apocryphal writings there are passages whose beautiful touching shows how just was the appreciation the nation had of their great leader, of which Eccl. xlv. may be taken as a chief instance. In the legend in 2 Macc. ii. (see also Mischna, 'de die expiationis.' Surenhusii), of the hiding of the tables of the law by Jeremiah in a cave in Mount Nebo, we may note with what historical sobriety and matter-of-fact treatment the past of Moses was handled, and yet the beginning of a vague expectation as to his future mission. At the same time it bears witness—incidentally—to the jealous caution with which memorials of him were regarded by the spiritual leaders.

When we come to Philo's life of Moses, we find an evidently artificial fabric. Incidents are drawn out and motives of action attributed with a precision which is, of necessity, but imagined ; while at places the narration suddenly drops from the supernatural level into philosophic rationalising. The early life of Moses in the hands of such merely patriotic writers contrasts most suggestively with the pure Scripture. Philo, aiming at superiority over the Egyptians as well as the Greeks, would make out that Moses was surreptitiously passed off by the royal princess as her own child, and that as such he came to be acknowledged heir to the Egyptian throne. Josephus, again, whose narrative is conceived in the same vein, regards the adoption as an open act, accepted by the king, and goes on to describe the monarch as putting his crown, in sport, on the child's head, and the child as dashing it to the ground ; the sacred scribe as regarding the omen unfavourably, and striving on the spot to kill Moses. This author also gives a circumstantial account of a war which he says Moses led for Egypt against the Ethiopians, and of his completing it by a sudden marriage with the king of Ethiopia's enamoured daughter; and he attributes the fall of Moses to the jealousy of the priests, who feared his too great power. Philo, on the other hand, gives as its occasion, the death of the Egyptian, spoken of in the Scripture, and the jealousy of the king whom he describes as worked on by the courtiers to apprehend Moses would depose him that he might himself reign before his time. The elaborate view of Moses' action in relation to the Hebrew Law, given by these two writers is, however, of great value for exposi-tion, and Philo's is especially important in connection with St. Paul's writings ; but the hazardous tone of their statements and conjectures in comparison with the pru-d nt reserve of Scripture, and their constant substitution of motives of policy for the higher springs and princi-ples avowed in the Bible, commends to us, even at a glance, the inspired narrative as much as would whole volumes of pleadings.

In the early Christian apologists Moses retains the full eminence of his position, and is freely used by them in comparisons with the Heathen sages. Justin Martyr quotes to the Greeks Philo and Josephus as authorities acceptable by them, and also their own Diodorus who shows Moses a great and memorable man and lawgiver, and who declares that it was he first persuaded the public to use written laws and to live by them. He even quotes a Greek oracle against the Greeks, admitting true wisdom to be found among the Chaldeans and Hebrews alone, since they alone are αὐτογένητον ἄνακτα σεβαζόμενοι Θεὸν ἁγνῶς, and appropriates this admission for the works of Moses. Clement Alex., in his 'Miscellanies,' also relates the early history of Moses, though with legends of dignity, as that Moses taught letters to the Jews, from whom they passed to the Phœnicians and Greeks; that he was by some said to have slain the Egyptian with the word of his mouth, as Peter did Ananias; that imprisoned, he stood before the king by night, and revealing the name of his God, the monarch was struck senseless. All these he brings from sources accredited by the Greeks, and then he goes on to claim for Moses the tuition of the Greeks in politic wisdom, and describes him as the model Plato followed in legislation.

Origen made it his business to reply to Celsus who appears to have been a hardy opponent of Christianity, plainly asserting that the herdsmen and shepherds, followers of Moses, had been deluded by vulgar impositions, and so become ensnared into the belief that there is but one God, and hinting that Moses having picked up the doctrine from wise nations and superior men, had got credit for being himself a sort of divinity. Celsus went on, it seems, to name various nations as originators of great doctrines, but said not a word in the matter on the Jews. To this Origen, vindicating the Hebrew system, strongly retorts Celsus' own account of his own gods, and asks if it is a better account than that of Moses, and claims for the great legislator that his law was both a practical teaching for the people he led, and also a grand subject of speculation for the wise. He then contrasts the Egyptian with the Hebrew, and asks if it is reasonable to describe the latter as foolish for referring the world to one creator, and the former as wise, who make countless animals divine. He further presses the matter even against the Jews themselves in his pleading for Christ, and puts it 'two persons are credited with marvels beyond human power, Moses and Jesus. Moses you believe in, notwithstanding that the Egyptians declared him a sorcerer. Why are we to disbelieve Jesus, merely because you are his accusers?'

At the root of all these ancient discussions we may see the same impulse and effort to place the original source of knowledge on the side of the advocate, and the same common impression that to establish this would be to gain victory in the controversy. This perpetual yearning on all sides for an authoritative source of truth is an interesting discovery of the habitual and perhaps essential tendency of the human mind in such matters, and shows us clearly that it must be useful, and perhaps even necessary in any real communications

from heaven to the human race, to approach men by the
process by which alone they seem fully accessible : that
is, by such distinct initiatives and primary communications as would enable all to feel ' here is the final spring
and fountain-head of knowledge, and here therefore we
may rest.' The whole attitude of antiquity makes it
clear that inference is not sufficient basis for the convictions of men at large, in so great a concern as religion ;
but that they require and cannot dispense with full and
authoritative announcements of it, and that some such
work as the revelations and law of Moses is essential to
those active and permanent impressions which lead to
advancements of society and satisfy perpetually recurring
questions. Nor can we conclude without pointing out
how fairly the fact presses us, that the whole field of
evidence, from first to last, consistently and unaffectedly,
places Moses before us as a genuine historical personage.
One so distinctly historical, indeed, that the legendary
seems utterly unable to attach itself to him, so that he is
found gaining none of those accretions and developments
in passing through succeeding ages, which we observe
collecting round the heroes of heathenism, but remains at
the last, after fulfilling the most exalted functions, in precisely the same biographical attitude as at the beginning
of Scripture. From this the inference is obvious that the
attempt to charge his surroundings with mythical elements must be regarded as a failure.

PAGE 152.

The Hardening of Pharaoh's Heart.—While the
inner workings of divine Providence are here described,

they are yet in full accordance with its outer and ordinary manifestations. Ewald, in his effort to explain
away the supernatural, clearly shows the naturalness of
the movement. He describes the king as 'driven by the
consequences of his former injustice against the people,'
as 'relying in the might of wrong, in its supposed
supports, and in some apparent successes,' as becoming
thus more and more hardened, and then, when these consequences of his conduct return to him in ever-increasing chastisement, as remaining undecided, hoping
yet to retain the imagined benefit of the slave population; delaying, and yet at last obliged to yield—'an eternal, great type of the vain resistance to right and truth.'
We find in this typical case the ever-increasing inju-
riousness of sin persisted in, to the sinner. We see
by it also how such sin, while tolerated for mercy's
sake until full means of probation have been tried, is yet
all the time made to subserve counsels of goodness, so
that if God seem to work in vain with the one, He is
yet all the while working successfully with the many
through the one. We have in it very likely before us a
reflection of the inner mysteries of spiritual conflict.
We have also a declaration of the wide policy of tolerance in the outer sphere. 'And in very deed for this
cause have I raised thee up for to show in thee my
power, and that my name may be declared throughout
all the earth.' (הֶעֱמַדְתִּיךָ, I have enabled thee to endure,
i.e., to live on and persist until the divine plans shall
have been worked out).

Passing to antiquity we find the early Christian apologists, in opposition to the heretics of their day who

aimed at establishing a Demiurge, or world governor of
the Old Testament, distinct from and inferior to the God
of the New Testament, maintaining the essential identity
of all Scripture, and from their point of controversy vindicating the justice and mercy of God in the Old Testament transaction. Irenæus, *Contra Heræs.* iv. 28, 29,
reminds them that the same facts repeat themselves as
part of the general dealing of God in both covenants
alike; and that as Israel was saved by the blindness
of Pharaoh, so the Christians are by the blindness of
the Jews. For the same divine counsels, he holds, are
ever to different persons diversely, 'a savour of death
unto death, or a savour of life unto life.' 2 Cor. ii. 15.
As God dealt with Pharaoh, so our Lord spoke to the
Jews in parables, though to His own Christian children plainly, that hearing, these former might not hear,
according to the word of Isaiah, 'make the heart of this
people gross,' Matt. xiii. 2. Isai. vi. 10 ; and this not
specially or of intent ; but even as the sun is painful to
those of weak eyes, while sweet and light-giving to
others. Where then, 'the god of this world has blinded
the eyes of them that believe not, lest the light of the
glorious gospel of Christ should shine unto them,'
2 Cor. iv. 4 ; there it was because 'they did not think
fit to have God in their knowledge, that God gave them
up to a reprobate mind.' Rom. i. 28. The causing of
which state is not the work of Christ but of Antichrist ;
and then because they are found in this state God is
sending to them, the 'working of error in order that
they should believe the falsehood.' 2 Thess. ii. 11, which
means, God at last leaves men still in the darkness

they have themselves finally chosen by the prompting of
Satan; and so likewise it is only in accordance with
God's general dealing in all Scripture that He should
also leave Pharaoh, who never did or would have believed,
and this leaving is called ' hardening him.'

Tertullian, in confuting Marcion (ii. 14), leader in the
false teaching that the Demiurgus, or Creator, is not the
Supreme God, and that Matter, which he considered co-
eternal with God, is essentially evil, also takes up the
case of Pharaoh. The Marcionites insisted that the Old
Testament God acknowledged Himself the Author of
evil. ' It is I who create evil ;' but, says Tertullian,
there are evils culpæ and evils pœnæ, the former bad
morally, but the latter remedial. Those wilfully de-
spising good are not unjustly punished. Pharaoh earned
it, to be so dealt with as to lead to his destruction,
and when God's own people were persistently ungrate-
ful, neither did they escape, though in all severe dealings
it is to be remembered there is ever in the divine counsels something remedial, and if we trace God's government in history, we shall ever find it full of this goodness.

The case of Pharaoh is reasoned very fully by Origen
(de Princip. iii. 1), in connection with the question of
Free Will. He puts it thus. If there was, according to
their adverse contention, a fatalistic necessity in Pharaoh's
nature to act as he did, what was the meaning of his heart
being hardened, which it was several times. The very
expression that he hardened himself implies he might on
the other hand have yielded ; and he insists that by one
and the same act God has pity on one and hardens another, not purposing that he who is hardened should be so,

but bringing out by his very compassion, forbearance, and delay, the impenitent's contempt and insolent perseverance in evil. Wherein his blessing is like the rain, which is a calling forth of good fruit in one land, while it serves only to bring out thorns and briars in another, 'whose end is to be burned.' Heb. vi. 7. The difference being that one land is dressed by the husbandman, and the other neglected. From one point of view it is the rain on which the good fruits and the weeds are dependent, but from another it is, with equal truth, the labour or neglect. So every one's will if unsubdued, is hardened by the very dealings which, when the will is subdued, will help obedience. Further, it is evident the hardening of Pharaoh is not of such a nature as some take it to be, for in that case he would not have given way at all; but there was some impression, though it was resisted, and this resistance was from his inner state; so that grace here was like the sun, which, while it softens wax, hardens mud. To Pharaoh, then, are to be applied the words of St. Paul, Rom. ii. 4. 'Despisest thou the riches of his goodness and forbearance and long-suffering, not knowing that the goodness of God leadeth thee to repentance, but after thy hardness and impenitent heart, treasurest up unto thyself wrath.'

Augustine in his 'Sermons for the Seasons' (*Serm.* 88), also goes into the case at length. He describes the remaining in sin as bringing desperation, desperation as bringing obduracy, and obduracy a contempt of the long-suffering which gives time for repentance, thus treasuring up wrath. In this way hardness comes from the very forbearance of God, not from His severity. So when the Lord is said to harden Pharaoh's heart it is as if it were said, 'I have suspended my plagues and so allowed him to harden his heart.' Thus Isaiah i. 5, 'Why should ye be stricken any more? ye will revolt more and more.' Pharaoh was bad through his past sins, and therefore let alone. So we read concerning God's own people (Isa. lxiii.), 'In His love and His pity He redeemed them; but they rebelled and vexed His holy spirit, therefore He was turned to be their enemy:' and then, 'O Lord, why hast Thou made us to err from Thy ways, and hardened our heart from Thy fear.' Indeed Pharaoh himself sees the case better than do the 'immundissimi Manichæi,' for he owns that the Lord is just, and he and his people sinners. See also Quæst. super Exod. xxiv., and Ps. cxviii. 18, immediately after the captivity of Babylon, where as the end of the works and mighty doings of Jehovah and His chastening, His real servants are 'not given over to death.'

In Jerome, vol. ix. 70, the same general position is found; and also in his comment on Isaiah, c. vi., is some consideration of those deeper aspects of the subject which have not here been entered on. Among many of our own writers, Tillotson, speaking on such judgments, says, 'the sin of Pharaoh was also the reproach of Israel.' 'The people turneth not to Him that smiteth them, neither do they seek the Lord of Hosts.' (Isa. ix. 13). This was the brand of Ahaz, that 'in the time of his distress he trespassed yet more against the Lord' (2 Chron. xxviii. 22), and he it was who was said to have provoked the Lord, more than all the kings of Israel which were before Him.' See ' Tillotson's Serm. xxxii.; Hooker V., Appendix i. ; Hammond's Sermon, ' God's complaint against revolters,' &c.

Ark of The Covenant a Type of Christ.—'Arca constructa erat in modum cistæ, intrinsecus atque extrinsecus auro obducta: repræsentans Christi puritatem, in cogitationibus internis simul et externis actionibus. Pedibus, quibus niteretur, carebat, fundo suo insistens solo, inque eo figura Christi humiliantis se super terram. Extrinsecus super supremam oram factus erat aureus Limbus circumquaque formâ coronariâ, repræsentans, inquiunt Judæi, coronam Legis, sed aptissimè Christum coronatum gloriâ. Singulis angulis inditi erant annuli Aurei, in quos inducti erant duo vectes è lignis Cedrorum lectissimarum Auro obducti, quibus Arca portaretur, mansuri istic perpetuò et nunquam amovendi; quo, ut quidam exponunt, Sacerdotes monebantur, ut parati semper et præstò adessent ad ministerium; sed potiùs eo adumbrata videtur Christi Deitas, humanitatem ejus sustentans, nullo unquam tempore ab ipso recessura. Operculum in veteri simul et Novo Testamento dicitur Propitiatorium, Anglis vulgò *Mercy-Seat*; atque ita nuncupatur, quià Deus inde gratiosè populo suo est locutus. Hanc partem benè attende, et plenè videbis Christum.' (Lightfoot, *Spicilig. in Exod.* xxxvii.) The above may, perhaps, overstrain to some extent in the effort to secure resemblances, but it will serve to show, at any rate, that this general idea with regard to the typical meaning of the Ark was favoured by a writer familiar with the details of Hebrew antiquity, and with their relations to the Gospel.

Page 283.

Moses Interceding, a Type of Christ's Intercessory Work.—'Deus in ipsâ etiam ferociâ suâ, cùm ob vituli consecrationem efferatus in populum, de famulo suo postulat Moyse, "Sine me et in irâ disperdam illos, et faciam te in nationem magnam." Unde meliorem soletis affirmare Moysen Deo suo, deprecatorem, immo et prohibitorem iræ. Non facies enim, inquit, istud, aut et me unà cum eis impende. Miserandi vos quoque cum populo, qui Christum non agnoscitis in personâ Moysis figuratum, Patris deprecatorem, et oblatorem animæ suæ pro populi salute. Sed sufficit, si et Moysi propriè donatus est populus ad præsens; quod ut famulus postulare posset à domino, id dominus à se postulavit. Ad hoc enim famulo dixit, "Sine me et disperdam illos, ut ille postulando, et semetipsum offerendo non sineret; atque ita disceres quantum liceat fideli et Prophetæ apud Deum." (Tertull. *adv. Marcionem*, ii. 26.) We may say then that, while in leading out the people, in legislating for them, in patiently bearing their burden, and in many details, Moses was a type; in few points, if any, did he more eminently prefigure the 'prophet like unto himself' than in this central act of prevailing intercession for repentant sinners.

LONDON : PRINTED BY
SPOTTISWOODE AND CO., NEW-STREET SQUARE
AND PARLIAMENT STREET

LECTURES

ON

EARLY SCRIPTURE.

BY REV. DR. CROSSE.

Price 5s.

London : LONGMANS, GREEN, and CO. Paternoster Row.
May be had of all Booksellers.

LONDON QUARTERLY REVIEW.

'A wise and thoughtful book, which the reader of Scripture and the student of science may both handle with advantage. Without attempting any formal solution of the difficulties arising out of the new relations of science and the written revelation, Dr. Crosse shows that the position held by the Bible in the controversy is as far as possible from being the hopeless one which some of its scientific opponents assume it to be ; that, in point of fact, the great religious and historical affirmations of early Scripture are still the only rational account which can be given of the matters to which they refer ; and that there is a harmony, not to say an identity, between the doctrines of the most ancient and of the latest parts of the Bible which is not to be explained, except on the principle that it is what the Christian Church believes it to be—the supernaturally inspired Word of God. This argument runs through Dr. Crosse's volume, and is managed with much moderation, tact, and quiet force. At the same time the Author finds occasion to string upon his main thread, always appropriately and gracefully, abundance of acute and sensible observations on the special topics of his Lectures.'

CHURCHMAN.

'The fact that these clear and well-written Lectures have already reached a second edition almost precludes the necessity of saying a great deal in their praise. They are emphatically sensible. Without pretentiousness, they yet give in a straightforward and intelligible way the results both of thought and reading.'

LITERARY CHURCHMAN.

'The volume before us, though dealing with a hackneyed subject, is as unhackneyed as it is possible to be ; its whole tone and contents as fresh and vigorous as if it were the first reply that had ever been rendered. . . . In the most delicately skilful and impartially convincing way conceivable, and without a trace of that too often bitter war of words which one is accustomed to in ordinary controversial treatises, the strongholds of the sceptic are seen first to totter from very baselessness, and then altogether to crumble away when tried with the touchstone of truth. . . . Dr. Crosse has brought to his subject a refinement of taste, and delicacy of touch, which make his book as elegant and pleasing as it is suggestive; while there is a clear vein of common sense and a dignified soberness pervading the whole which should make it especially acceptable to those for whom it was intended—the enlightened and educated inquirers and students of this nineteenth century. We commend it most heartily to the attention of all our readers.'

GUARDIAN.

'Dr. Crosse's Lectures on Early Scripture have deservedly reached a second edition. The scope of the volume may be said generally to be to claim for Scripture to be judged by the light of its own avowed purposes, and to point out its wonderful aptness and truth when so judged. There is sufficient both of originality and power in the execution of this design to take the work out of the category of mere sermons, and to give it a more lasting value.'

BRITISH AND FOREIGN EVANGELICAL REVIEW.

'We have been arrested and charmed by the perusal of this volume. It is replete with original thought, profound reflection, and striking argument. The sentiments of the writer are sound and evangelical, but what has specially delighted us in perusing these Lectures is to see a mind so richly imbued with the spirit of genuine philosophy bowing with such profound reverence before the shrine of Holy Scripture, and bringing it out in harmony with the wisdom, power, and goodness of God. In an age when our would-be philosophers seem to take a pride and pleasure in finding out discrepancies between Scripture and science, it is truly refreshing to see such a writer as Dr. Crosse, at once a scholar, a lawyer, and a divine, devoting his energies to the noble task not merely of vindicating Scripture, but by placing it in its true light, commending it to the admiration and homage of mankind. We shall await with much interest the promised sequel of these valuable Lectures.'

In the press.

BY THE SAME AUTHOR.

LECTURES ON HEBREW LAW.

Spottiswoode & Co., Printers, New-street Square and 30 Parliament Street.